D1829373

SHROPSHIRE CURIOSITIES

GEORGE GLOVER has spent most of his life in Shropshire. His articles on the county's curiosities appeared in the 'Out and About' column of early editions of *The Shropshire Star* and he has written three published operettas. A teacher for 35 years, he is now the vice-chairman of the Shropshire Talking Newspaper.

ROBERT JONES lives in Herefordshire and makes hand-painted ceramic tiles.

75 The Refectory Pulpit

SHROPSHIRE CURIOSITIES

George Glover

with drawings by

Robert Jones

ARCH

© George Glover 1989

Drawings © Robert Jones 1989

Published by ARCH, Lower Grantsfield,
Kimbolton, Leominster, Herefordshire HR6 OET

Cover photograph: Christopher Morris

Photoset in Mergenthaler Bembo and Centaur
at Five Seasons Press, Madley, Hereford

Printed and bound in Great Britain
by Billings and Sons Limited, Worcester

British Library Catologuing in Publication Data
(a CIP catalogue record for this book
is available from the British Library)

ISBN 0 947618 04 X

Contents

Acknowledgements

I would like to acknowledge the contribution made to the compilation of this book by my son David and his wife Evi. Thanks also to my wife Joan, who read the manuscript. Their help and enthusiasm have been invaluable.

A Note on the Illustrations

A number of the illustrations in this book are reproduced as a series of hand-painted ceramic tiles. Further details are available from Jones' Tiles, Orelton Manor, Ludlow, Shropshire SY8 4HR. Telephone: 056885 666.

The Publishers would like to acknowledge the co-operation and help of Shropshire County Council.

SHROPSHIRE

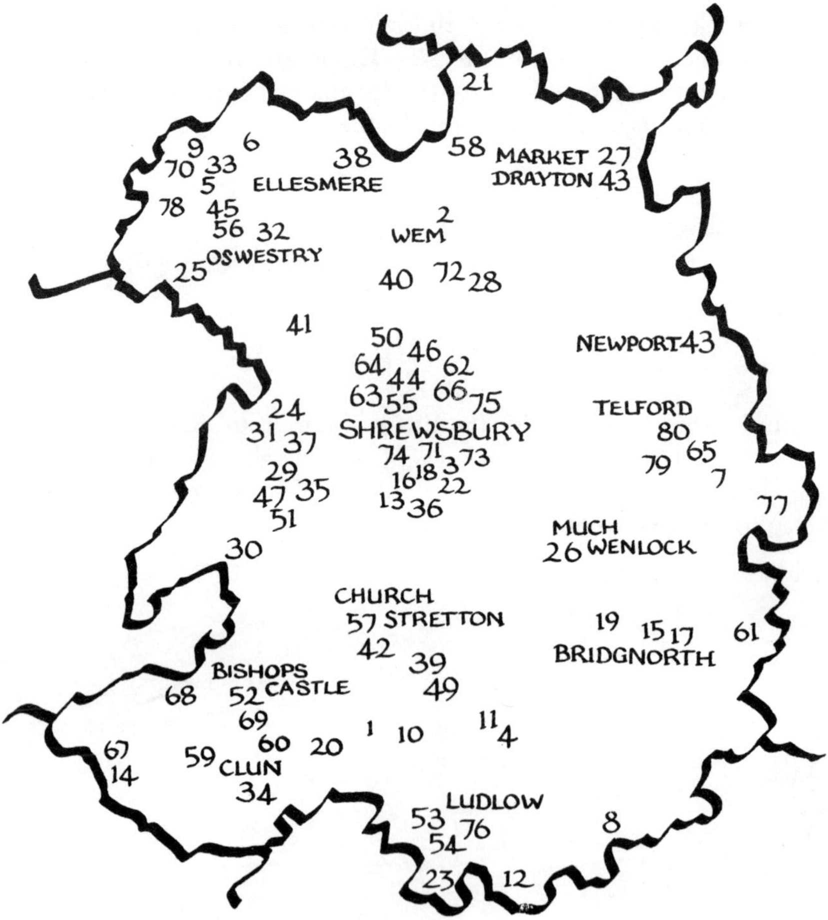

21
9
6
70
33
5
38
ELLESMERE
58
MARKET DRAYTON
27
43
78
45
56
32
2
WEM
OSWESTRY
25
40
72
28
41
50
46
NEWPORT
43
64
62
44
63
55
66
75
24
TELFORD
31
37
SHREWSBURY
80
74
71
3
73
65
79
29
18
16
22
7
47
35
13
36
77
51
MUCH WENLOCK
26
30
CHURCH STRETTON
57
19
15
17
61
BRIDGNORTH
42
39
BISHOPS CASTLE
68
52
49
69
11
1
10
4
60
20
67
59
CLUN
14
34
LUDLOW
53
76
8
54
23
12

Introduction

In assembling this collection of Shropshire curiosities I have tried to avoid the best-known guide-book favourites and to encourage the sightseer to get out and about in some of the lesser-known parts of the county. None of the suggested items involves substantial admission charges.

A number of Shropshire's most celebrated curiosities are in private hands, and many of the follies, alas! have been allowed to disintegrate beyond recognition. But there is still enough left, especially in churches, to satisfy the average curiosity-seeker for a long summer of fine weekends.

1 Flounder's Folly

POSITION: On the summit of Callow Hill, at the southern end of Wenlock Edge.

ORDNANCE MAP: Landranger 137. Ludlow, Wenlock Edge etc.

MAP REF: SO461851

ACCESS: Difficult unless you can read the OS map. Take the B4368 out of Craven Arms in the direction of Much Wenlock. In a little over a quarter of a mile turn left for the village of Halford and, after a further quarter of a mile, right for Lower Dinchope (about 1½ miles), where you should bear left for Westhope. A mile from Lower Dinchope, where the road bends sharply left (map ref. 459852), a track leads to the right towards the woods on the side of Callow Hill. From here the right-of-way involves an ascent on your hands and knees, and a descent on your backside, especially after rain.

¶ An alternative route, which allows the climb to be made with greater dignity, although it's a lot further and much less of a challenge, involves following the B4368 to Culmington Manor, about three miles from Craven Arms, from where a two-mile-long footpath leads up to the Folly.

NOTE: The tower was put up by one Benjamin Flounder in 1839, and is said to mark the spot where four estates met, and perhaps still do. At 1,112 feet it is the highest point on Wenlock Edge, and a conspicuous landmark.

¶ It was built as a look-out tower, from which Benjamin, who must have had remarkable eyesight, is said to have been able to see his ships in dock at Liverpool. He was a Quaker, alleged to have been partial to hunting, shooting, and drinking port wine.

¶ There are superb views from the Folly, including Ludlow and the Welsh Hills.

PLACES OF INTEREST IN THE NEIGHBOURHOOD

20. The Arbor Tree (Aston-on-Clun)
49. The Rude Lady (Holdgate)

FOOD AND ACCOMMODATION

In Craven Arms.

2 A Superb Norman Doorway

POSITION: Edstaston

ORDNANCE MAP: Landranger 126. Shrewsbury, etc.

MAP REF: SJ518320

ACCESS: From the B5476, 2 miles north of Wem, an unclassified road leads you in a quarter of a mile to the church, which is beside the road, on your right.

NOTE: The old church was a mere chapel until 1850, when it was upgraded. It has two very good Norman doorways, the best in Shropshire. It is believed that the doors themselves, and the accompanying ironwork, are original.

¶The better of the two is the north doorway, which has five splendid orders. The carving has weathered remarkably well.

PLACES OF INTEREST IN THE NEIGHBOURHOOD

58. The Van Gogh Canal Bridge (Tilstock)
38. Prince Moshueshue's Grave (Welshampton)

FOOD AND ACCOMMODATION

Wem can provide.

3 The Parliamentary Gable Ends

POSITION: Acton Burnell

ORDNANCE MAP: Landranger 126 Shrewsbury, etc.

MAP REF: SJ535019

ACCESS: From the Weeping Cross roundabout on the A5 two miles south of Shrewsbury take the unclassified road almost due south through Cantlop and Pitchford to Acton Burnell. At the cross roads in the village turn left, then right before the gates of Concord College to park opposite the church. Walk a little further up the lane, go through the pedestrian gate on your left and along the path through the trees. Pass the castle, and the gable ends are on the College playing fields in front of you.

NOTE: The stone barn gable ends, if that is what they really are, stand 157 feet apart and are 40 feet wide at the base. Many historians hold that these are the remains of the barn where the first English Parliament sat in the year 1283 and passed the Statute of Acton Burnell. This required all debtors in London, York and Bristol to meet their respective mayors and fix a date for payment. Failure to do this would result in the debtors' property being confiscated.

PLACES OF INTEREST IN THE NEIGHBOURHOOD

22. Acton Burnell Castle
73. The Burnell Burnished Brass
36. Langley Chapel

FOOD AND ACCOMMODATION

A wide choice at Shrewsbury, 7 miles to the north.

4 The Lonely Norman Chapel

POSITION: Heath

ORDNANCE MAP: Landranger 138. Kidderminster & Wyre Forest.

MAP REF: SO557856

ACCESS: Whichever way you approach, it's a matter of good map reading. The chapel is on the western slope of Brown Clee hill, between Tugford and Clee St. Margaret. It stands in a field, and the key, a notice on the iron gates tells you, is obtainable from a farm 340 yards away.

NOTE: Words like perfect, beautiful, alone, lonely, remote, simple, humble, plain and primitive have all been used by guidebook writers to describe it. It's eleventh-century, and little has been done to alter the original fabric. There is neither tower nor belfry.

¶ The interior is whitewashed. The furnishings, most of them from the seventeenth-century, include box-pews and a double-decker pulpit.

¶ Behind the chapel may be discerned the tell-tale outlines of a deserted village. There are many such in the county, particularly in scattered communities like this.

PLACES OF INTEREST IN THE NEIGHBOURHOOD

11. Where a Village Street is Permanently under Water

49. The Rude Lady

FOOD AND ACCOMMODATION

Various local public-houses, or Ludlow or Craven Arms.

5 The Italian Station

POSITION: Gobowen

ORDNANCE MAP: Landranger 126. Shrewsbury, etc.

MAP REF: SJ303334

ACCESS: Two miles north of Oswestry, in Gobowen village, with a level crossing on the Shrewsbury–Chester line.

NOTE: At the junction with the former short feeder link from Oswestry, the station declined in importance when that shuttle service was closed down. In recent years the buildings were allowed to deteriorate, becoming sadly shabby. Local agitation has led to the restoration by British Rail of this building of unusual architectural interest.

¶It is claimed that a quarter of a million pounds has been spent on refurbishment and the result, especially seen in sunshine, is quite splendid.

¶The station is Italianate in style, and has been finished in pale grey, trimmed with green, white, and deep pink.

PLACES OF INTEREST IN THE NEIGHBOURHOOD

9. Four Ways to Cross a Valley (Chirk)
45. Old Oswestry (Oswestry)
78. Oswald's Well (Oswestry)

FOOD AND ACCOMMODATION

Gobowen and Oswestry.

6 A Venerable Churchyard Yew

POSITION: Dudleston

ORDNANCE MAP: Landranger 126. Shrewsbury, etc.

MAP REF: SJ346385

ACCESS: The unclassified roads to the hamlet of Dudleston can be identified from the B5068 (Ellesmere–St. Martin's) and the B5069 (St. Martin's–Overton-on-Dee) roads. But the place should not be confused with Dudleston Heath, a daughter parish which has outgrown its mother. St Mary's church, signposted off a quiet road later, stands on quite high ground, from which there are panoramic views towards the Welsh Mountain outliers and over the Cheshire plain.

NOTE: This ancient yew was probably already growing before the Norman Conquest. It stands outside the main, west door of the church, and is only one of several around the churchyard. Its loins have been girded for at least half a century with an iron strap, and time was when choirboys used to hide in its hollow trunk.

¶It is on record that when the church tower was under repair in the last century the single bell was hung and rung from a robust upper branch in this tree.

¶If the church is open, don't fail to admire the east window and, at the back of the church, a splendid chest cut from a solid piece of oak.

PLACES OF INTEREST IN THE NEIGHBOURHOOD

33. Church Furniture of the Past (St. Martin's)
70. A Stonehenge Folly (Weston Rhyn)
9. Four Ways to Cross a Valley (Chirk)

7 The Matthew Webb Monument

POSITION: High Street, Dawley.

ORDNANCE MAP: Landranger 127. Stafford, Telford, etc.

MAP REF: SJ688073

NOTE: Considering that Webb's feat in being the first person to swim the English Channel was acclaimed by the whole nation, and in many other countries besides, this memorial is rather disappointing. In these days, of course, Channel swimming has become almost commonplace. Dawley has given this fountain, with its small bronze portrait, a place of honour in its shopping centre. There is another memorial, with a better representation of the then national hero, near the spot where Webb emerged after his epic swim.

¶The story of his life is rather sad. The hero found the gradual waning of public interest difficult to live with. So, for a wager, he accepted a challenge to swim the rapids in the Niagara River, a short distance below the Falls. Those of us who have walked beside the turbulent, rock-strewn waters can feel no surprise that it proved fatal for the gallant swimmer. But he was the first, as far as we know, to swim the English Channel, and nobody can take that away from him—even though the inscription on the monument puts his life-saving feats before the epic swim.

PLACES OF INTEREST IN THE NEIGHBOURHOOD

79. The Mary Tooth Tomb

FOOD AND ACCOMMODATION

Take your pick in Telford.

8 The Twisted Spire

POSITION: Cleobury Mortimer

ORDNANCE MAP: Landranger 138. Kidderminster & Wyre Forest.

MAP REF: SO674758

ACCESS: The Church of St. Mary the Virgin in Cleobury Mortimer is beside the A4117 road, 11 miles from Bewdley, 14 miles from Bridgnorth, 12 miles from Ludlow.

NOTE: The first thing you notice about the church as you approach it is the crooked spire, set upon a square tower. It is made of wood, covered in wooden shingles, and broached.
¶ It's not only the spire which is out of true. The walls, too, lean at crazy angles, and an ancient Norman arch is looking its age.

PLACES OF INTEREST IN THE NEIGHBOURHOOD
12. The Cornwall Triptych (Burford)
53. The Face at The Feathers (Ludlow)

FOOD AND ACCOMMODATION
In the town.

9 Four Ways to Cross a Valley

POSITION: Chirk

ORDNANCE MAP: Landranger 126. Shrewsbury, etc.

MAP REF: SJ287372

ACCESS: Best approached from Chirk Bank, where the unclassified road to Weston Rhyn takes you in a very short distance to the canal bridge, where there is room to park. Now stroll along a pleasant tree-shaded towpath beside the 'cut' towards the border. You will emerge on the aqueduct itself, with the railway line above you on your left.

NOTE: For nearly 200 years Telford's aqueduct carrying the canal has spanned the Ceiriog Valley. It is 200 yards long and has 10 arches, each with a span of 40 feet, 70 feet above the floor of the valley. After that sentence full of figures, you should pause to appreciate that it was a considerable feat of engineering.
¶The company which sponsored the structure could not have suspected that only 50 years later the concept would be challenged by the arrival of a competitor, a viaduct carrying a railway, parallel to the aqueduct, but 30 feet higher. That structure, built by Thomas Brassey, has 15 arches of 45 feet span, and is 283 yards long.
¶Far below is the road. If you are patient enough, you can see international traffic moving on three levels. Bearing in mind that the towpath is a foot or so above the water, you have four ways of crossing without taking to the air! (You will also walk from England into Wales halfway across.)
¶If you don't suffer from vertigo and are able to stroll across the aqueduct you can carry on through a dark and dripping tunnel to emerge near the old Chirk railway station.

PLACES OF INTEREST IN THE NEIGHBOURHOOD
6. A Venerable Churchyard Yew (Dudleston)
33. Church Furniture of the Past (St. Martin's)

FOOD AND ACCOMMODATION
In Chirk.

10 The Painted Ceiling

POSITION: Bromfield

ORDNANCE MAP: Landranger 137. Ludlow, Wenlock Edge etc.

MAP REF: SO482768

ACCESS: St. Mary's Church, Bromfield, is 3 miles north-west of Ludlow, quite close to the A49 Shrewsbury road and to the confluence of the rivers Teme and Onny.

NOTE: This rather maltreated church used to be part of a Priory, whose sorry gatehouse, its neglected timbers bleached to grey, still stands. After the Dissolution a certain Charles Foxe converted part of the buildings, including the central tower, into a house. In 1672, when the old tower became the new chancel of the re-fashioned church, Thomas Francis decorated its ceiling with this curious painting.

¶ Opinions about its quality are polarised. Some see it as a good example of the worst kind of ecclesiastical art. Others declare it to be 'a most encouraging piece of folk art'. What do you think?

¶ Do not miss the stone plaque to H. H. Hickman, surgeon (1800–30), and be thankful for his pioneer work in anaesthesia.

PLACES OF INTEREST IN THE NEIGHBOURHOOD

54. The Hexagonal Porch
76. Where the Shropshire Lad at last found Peace
53. The Face at The Feathers

FOOD AND ACCOMMODATION

Adequate in Ludlow.

11 Where a Village Street is Permanently under Water

POSITION: Clee St. Margaret

ORDNANCE MAP: Landranger 138. Kidderminster & Wyre Forest.

MAP REF: SO565844

ACCESS: The OS map is useful! From the B4364 Ludlow–Bridgnorth road an unclassified road leads north from Lodge Cott, about 4½ miles from Ludlow. After a mile or so, a left turn leads to Stoke St. Milborough. The road which takes you straight through the village, avoiding the road which bears left, reaches Clee St. Margaret after a further 1½ miles or so.
¶ For those with an even better-developed taste for narrow lanes and frequent pauses at signposts, Clee St. Margaret can be reached through attractive countryside from the B4368 Craven Arms–Much Wenlock road. One route leads from Diddlebury through Reaton, Bouldon and Heath and another from Shipton through Stanton Long, Holdgate, Tugford and Abdon.

NOTE: The Clee Brook runs for 50 yards over the whole width of the road, after which it flings itself over a miniature precipice.
¶ The church is intriguing, too, with its low Norman doorway, its odd chancel arch with a rectangular hole on either side, its herringbone masonry and its squint. But it is the ford the visitor remembers most clearly.

PLACES OF INTEREST IN THE NEIGHBOURHOOD
49. The Rude Lady (Holdgate)

FOOD AND ACCOMMODATION
Ludlow or Craven Arms.

12 The Cornwall Triptych

POSITION: Burford

ORDNANCE MAP: Landranger 138. Kidderminster & Wyre Forest.

MAP REF: SO583680

ACCESS: St. Mary's Church lies about 500 yards south of the A456 road between Brimfield and Tenbury Wells, and about a mile from the latter. It is close to the left bank of the River Teme, which here forms the boundary between Shropshire and Herefordshire.

NOTE: The Cornwalls were barons of Burford for more than 400 years, and occupied Burford Castle, roughly where Burford House now stands.

¶The triptych, a rare Elizabethan example, is against the north wall of the chancel. If you are able to open the large doors you will find a painting by an artist by the name of Melchior Saboss. It depicts a Shropshire giant, Richard Cornwall, who stood 7 feet 3 inches tall, and who died in 1568. With him are figures thought to be his parents; an echelon of the heavenly army floats above. The central figure's walking-stick, initialled, leans against a nearby wall.

¶There were other interesting members of the family. One of the four Shropshire wooden effigies is here—an Edmund Cornwall, who died in 1508 at the age of 20.

¶There is a heart tomb as well, to the memory of another Edmund Cornwall, who died in Cologne. Before he succumbed he bade his servant bury his body there, but encase his heart in lead and take it back to Burford with him.

¶Finally, there is a note about a lady called Elenor, daughter of him who died in Cologne. She is reputed to have had 340 descendants before she died.

PLACES OF INTEREST IN THE NEIGHBOURHOOD

76. Where the Shropshire Lad at Last found Peace (Ludlow)
54. The Hexagonal Porch
23. The Vesica Window (Ashford Carbonell)

FOOD AND ACCOMMODATION

A good choice at Ludlow.

13 A Modest Telford Bridge

POSITION: Cantlop

ORDNANCE MAP: Landranger 126. Shrewsbury, etc.

MAP REF: SJ 518062

ACCESS: The most direct way is from the Weeping Cross traffic island on the A5 Shrewsbury by-pass. Drive almost due south for 1½ miles, then bear right when you have passed Betton Abbots and Betton Pool on your right. Straight across two crossroads on this unclassified road, and you cannot fail to spot the bridge on your left. There is a sensible parking area, picnic site and English Heritage notice.

NOTE: The bridge is described as the sole surviving example of a cast iron highway bridge designed by the celebrated Shropshire civil engineer Thomas Telford. So it's a scheduled Ancient Monument.

¶It was built in 1810, to carry the turnpike from Shrewsbury to Acton Burnell across the Cound Brook, and is to the same design as similar bridges at Meole Brace and Stokesay. While they have been replaced, this one is more or less in its original form.

PLACES OF INTEREST IN THE NEIGHBOURHOOD

71. The Condover Memorials (Condover)
22. Acton Burnell Castle
16. The Scarfaced Effigy (Berrington)

FOOD AND ACCOMMODATION

Back to Shrewsbury.

14 The Shepherds' Church

POSITION: Bettwys-y-Crwyn

ORDNANCE MAP: Landranger 137. Ludlow, Wenlock Edge etc.

MAP REF: SO206814

ACCESS: Difficult to find, this being a remote part of the Clun Forest. Starting from Clun, follow the B4368 westwards through Newcastle to Duffryn, where you should turn left along an unclassified road. Turn right at the first junction, then proceed more or less straight past Moor Hall, then uphill, ignoring a lane to the right and a cart-track to the left, until you spot the slate roof of the church.

NOTE: This is claimed to be one of the highest churches in England, at between 1400 and 1500 ft. The building dates from the thirteenth century and was built as a place of worship for the shepherds of the hills. It used to be thatched, and your attention is drawn to two holes on the exterior of the north wall where a pole was kept for dealing with a fire overhead.

¶ There is good Jacobean furniture; the most unusual feature is the farm names on the pew ends.

¶ The countryside hereabouts is wild and open, most attractive on a mild and sunny day. The map yields quaint names of tiny settlements—Quabbs, Twitchen, Beguildy, Spoad, Dawke, Hall of the Forest and Dingle-du-Bank.

PLACES OF INTEREST IN THE NEIGHBOURHOOD

68. Offa's Dyke (Mainstone)
67. The Cantlin Stone (Bettws-y-Crwyn)
59. A Quiet Church in a Quiet Town (Clun)

FOOD AND ACCOMMODATION

Clun, though a picnic near the Shepherds' Church might be the best bet.

15 The Tipsy Tower

POSITION: Bridgnorth

ORDNANCE MAP: Landranger 136 Kidderminster & Wyre Forest.

MAP REF: SO717927

ACCESS: From the south end of High Street in Bridgnorth go along West Castle Street to the castle precincts, or East Castle Street and around Telford's Church of St. Mary Magdalene.

NOTE: The 15° angle at which the ruin of the old keep leans can be quite alarming when you first see it—until you learn that it's been tilted like that for more than 350 years. The original damage was done when the powder magazine exploded in 1646, during the Civil War, the castle being under siege by Cromwell's men at the time.
¶ The castle was built in the twelfth century by Roger de Belesme, and the Castle Walk, declared King Charles I, afforded that monarch the finest view in his dominions. He knew how to please his hosts.

PLACES OF INTEREST IN THE NEIGHBOURHOOD
17. The Cliff Railway

FOOD AND ACCOMMODATION
Several restaurants and many public-houses in the town.

16 The Scarfaced Effigy

POSITION: All Saints' Church, Berrington

ORDNANCE MAP: Landranger 126. Shrewsbury, etc.

MAP REF: SJ531069

ACCESS: Proceed along the A458 from the Weeping Cross traffic island on the A5 Shrewsbury by-pass towards Bridgnorth and Kidderminster. At Cross Houses, after 2½ miles, turn right for Berrington village. When the village is reached, the church is then only a short distance along an unclassified road on your left.

NOTE: There are only about a hundred recumbent wooden effigies in the country. Shropshire has four of them. This chap, although perhaps not the best of the four, has a blemish on his face which resembles a scar.

¶The effigy, made of oak and dating from the thirteenth century, is in a recess in the south wall of the church. It represents a knight. The origin of the scar, if scar it is, is open to any interpretation the fanciful care to put on it. Local rumour had it at one time that the effigy commemorated a certain Owd Scriven, of Frodesley, who was on his way to see his sweetheart when a roaring lion attacked and mauled him. Not everybody was prepared to believe that story.

PLACES OF INTEREST IN THE NEIGHBOURHOOD

22. Acton Burnell Castle
73. The Burnell Burnished Brass (Acton Burnell)
13. A Modest Telford Bridge (Cantlop)
71. The Condover Memorials (Condover)

FOOD AND ACCOMMODATION

Cross Houses, Berrington.

17 The Cliff Railway

POSITION: Bridgnorth

ORDNANCE MAP: Landranger 138. Kidderminster & Wyre Forest.

MAP REF: SO711931

ACCESS: The top end is in Castle Hill Walk, and the bottom end in Underhill Street, almost opposite the old bridge over the River Severn.

NOTE: This funicular railway, opened in 1892, connects High Town with Low Town. It is the steepest and shortest cliff railway in England and nowadays the only inland cliff railway still working in Britain.
¶For more than 40 years it was hydraulically operated, but this system was superseded by electrically-operated winding gear in 1944. The railway, normally manned by two ladies, is a valuable alternative to the steep flights of 200 or so steps between the two levels in the town, especially for those afflicted by a walking disability, heavy shopping, or indolence.
¶If you take the short trip, which is mildly exciting, look out for Bishop Percy's house, a fine black-and-white building dated 1580, in the Cartway.
¶The return fare on the railway is currently 30p.

PLACES OF INTEREST IN THE NEIGHBOURHOOD
15. The Tipsy Tower (Bridgnorth)

FOOD AND ACCOMMODATION
Adequate in the town.

18 Where the Severn is Double-Crossed

POSITION: Atcham

ORDNANCE MAP: Landranger 126. Shrewsbury, etc.

MAP REF: SJ541093

ACCESS: Five miles south-west of Shrewsbury on the A5 (T) road.

NOTE: The main road from Shrewsbury to Telford and London is carried over the river Severn on a concrete bridge built in 1929. Alongside it is its predecessor, a fine old bridge opened in 1776, having been built by the architect John Gwynne. Gwynne was born in Shrewsbury. He designed the English Bridge, just four miles up the road, and the much-admired Magdalen Bridge in Oxford. His Atcham bridge, in Grinshill stone, was left in place when the newer one was brought into use, because of its pleasing design.

¶House martins have also found the bridge attractive. The old bridge, relieved of the pounding of modern traffic, has been taken over by one of the largest colonies of house martins in the country. Like Flanagan and Allen, they find agreeable shelter underneath the arches.

PLACES OF INTEREST IN THE NEIGHBOURHOOD
16. The Scarfaced Effigy (Berrington)
13. A Modest Telford Bridge (Cantlop)

FOOD AND ACCOMMODATION
The Mytton and Mermaid, in Atcham village, near the bridges. Plentiful in Shrewsbury.

19 Christ's Entry into Jerusalem

POSITION: Aston Eyre

ORDNANCE MAP: Landranger 138. Kidderminster & Wyre Forest.

MAP REF: SO653941

ACCESS: From Morville, on the A458 road between Much Wenlock and Bridgnorth, take the B4368 westwards towards Monkhopton. Aston Eyre church is a modest building about a mile along that road.

NOTE: The sculptured tympanum above the south door dates from the twelfth-century. It depicts Christ's entry into Jerusalem and is perhaps the finest piece of Norman sculpture in the county.
¶ Our Lord is shown seated on a rather long donkey with immense ears. On his right an old fellow is spreading palm branches for the beast to tread on. There is another man with an ass on the left.
¶ When we were at Aston Eyre last, English Heritage had put protective boarding over the sculpture, but this will presumably be removed when the porch roof has been repaired.

PLACES OF INTEREST IN THE NEIGHBOURHOOD

26. Built Fast, but Built to Last (Much Wenlock)
39. Wenlock Edge
15. The Tipsy Tower (Bridgnorth)
17. The Cliff Railway (Bridgnorth)

FOOD AND ACCOMMODATION

Bridgnorth, Much Wenlock

20 The Arbor Tree

POSITION: Aston-on-Clun

ORDNANCE MAP: Landranger 137. Ludlow, Wenlock Edge etc.

MAP REF: SO393817

ACCESS: About 3 miles from Craven Arms, on the B4368 road to Clun, it would be difficult to miss the Arbor Tree, always bedecked with flags, beside a bridge in the village.

NOTE: The rather battered old black poplar is dressed with a variety of flags fluttering or dangling from larch poles nailed to the tree.
¶ Tree-dressing, like well-dressing in Derbyshire and elsewhere, was a fertility rite. The custom is said to survive only in Aston-on-Clun. A festival, with pageant and dancing, takes place here annually on 29th May. Those of us brought up in other parts of rural Shropshire remember the date as Oak-apple Day, when children not wearing the obligatory oak-apple had their legs unmercifully 'nettled' for their sloth. The Arbor Tree, however, has a local significance unassociated with King Charles.
¶ It celebrates the wedding, as long ago as 1786, of John Marston and Mary Carter, popular young folk from nearby hamlets. The bride was so impressed by the villagers' tree-dressing, one version of the story goes, that she left money for the continuation of the annual revels, which have been carried on to the present day and seem likely to be maintained indefinitely.
¶ There are several variations of the basic story. Andrew Morton's *The Trees of Shropshire* is worth reading for further information on this delightful custom.

PLACES OF INTEREST IN THE NEIGHBOURHOOD
60. The Direction Pillar (Little Brampton)
52. The One-armed Clock (Lydbury North)

FOOD AND ACCOMMODATION
Craven Arms or Bishops Castle.

21 The Heart of the 'Scourge of France'

POSITION: Whitchurch

ORDNANCE MAP: Landranger 117. Chester.

MAP REF: SJ512417

ACCESS: St. Alkmund's church, with its high tower, stands on a hill and cannot be hid.

NOTE: Sir John Talbot was born near Whitchurch, and is renowned for his exploits in France during the Hundred Years War. Shakespeare wrote of him in *Henry VI, Part I:*

> The scourge of France, the Talbot so much feared
> That with his name the mothers still their babes.

He was killed in the thick of battle near Bordeaux in 1453.

¶ His heart was brought back to Whitchurch and buried in the porch of the church. The tomb, in the sanctuary, consists of an effigy with a great deal of information about his career and the honours and titles bestowed upon him. He was the first Earl of Shrewsbury, and the local grammar school was named after him.

¶ There is a remarkably good organ in the church; the case, with a trumpeting angel and heads of cherubs, should not be missed.

PLACES OF INTEREST IN THE NEIGHBOURHOOD.
58. A Van Gogh Bridge (Tilstock)

FOOD AND ACCOMMODATION.
In the town, hopefully.

22 Acton Burnell Castle

POSITION: Acton Burnell

ORDNANCE MAP: Landranger 126. Shrewsbury, etc.

MAP REF: SJ534019

ACCESS: See Access notes for No. 3 (The Barn Gable Ends). You walk past the castle on the way to that curiosity.

NOTE: Not a real castle, this roofless ruin was a fortified manor house. It was built by Robert Burnell, Bishop of Bath and Wells and Lord Chancellor to Edward I, in the 1280s. It is on flat ground, crenellated but without turrets, a large rectangular house with a round tower rising at each corner.
¶ Other families occupied the building after the last Burnell died in 1420. In the eighteenth century it is thought to have been used as a barn, and two elliptical arches were built into the long walls to admit high vehicles, perhaps loaded hay-carts.

PLACES OF INTEREST IN THE NEIGHBOURHOOD

3. The Parliamentary Gable Ends (Acton Burnell)
73. The Burnell Burnished Brass (Acton Burnell)
36. Langley Chapel (Langley)

FOOD AND ACCOMMODATION

Ample at Shrewsbury.

23 The Vesica Window

POSITION: Ashford Carbonell, Church of St. Mary Magdalene

ORDNANCE MAP: Landranger 137. Ludlow, Wenlock Edge etc.

MAP REF: SO625710

ACCESS: Leave the A49(T) by the signposted unclassified road three miles south of Ludlow. Then right at the first cross-roads beyond the attractive Teme bridge. The church is at the end of the first road on your left.

NOTE: The beautiful vesica window—a pointed oval—combines with two small lancet windows to present a most unusual group in the east wall.
¶The churchyard yews are worth more than a passing glance, a few of them being over 1,000 years old.

PLACES OF INTEREST IN THE NEIGHBOURHOOD
53. The Face at The Feathers (Ludlow)
76. Where the Shropshire Lad at Last found Peace (Ludlow)
54. The Hexagonal Porch (Ludlow)

FOOD AND ACCOMMODATION
In Ludlow.

24 The Prince's Oak

POSITION: Alberbury

ORDNANCE MAP: Landranger 126. Shrewsbury, etc.

MAP REF: SJ349146

ACCESS: Take the A458 (Welshpool) road from Shrewsbury to just beyond Ford (6 miles), and then a further 4 miles along the unclassified road towards Crewgreen. The oak is just beyond Alberbury, almost exactly on the Shropshire–Powys, that is, England–Wales border.

NOTE: The tree is not in itself outstanding as oak trees go in this district which used to supply timber for Britannia's fighting ships. But the Prince's Oak is easily identifiable by its protective wall and railings and explanatory plaque beside the road.

¶ The story is that in the late summer of 1806 the Prince of Wales, later King George IV, was staying with the Leightons at nearby Loton Park as a guest. One of the house-party suggested that this was a good opportunity for the Prince to visit his Principality. This he did, going through the park, crossing the border, and returning with a leafy sprig or two of oak stuck in his hat as a token of his brief visit.

¶ The protection now in place around the tree is perhaps the result of what happened to the King's Oak at Boscobel, where souvenir hunters hacked off pieces—in one case enough to make a chair—and the magnificent oak in Sherwood Forest, where a fence has had to be put up to prevent visitors' feet from compacting the earth, as the old giant wasn't getting enough rainwater to keep its canopy alive.

PLACES OF INTEREST IN THE NEIGHBOURHOOD

31. The Pastoral Church (Melverley)
41. The Highwayman who Lived with Beelzebub in a Cave (Nesscliffe)
35. An Unusual Church (Minsterley)

FOOD AND ACCOMMODATION

At Shrewsbury, where there is no lack.

25 The Church of Flowers

POSITION: Llanyblodwel

ORDNANCE MAP: Landranger 126. Shrewsbury, etc.

MAP REF: SJ239229

ACCESS: From Llynclys, four miles south of Oswestry, take the B4396 Llanfyllin road for about two miles, then turn right on to the Llangedwyn road (B4396) for half a mile and finally follow the brief signposted offshoot to this charming border village.

NOTE: The church is our main curiosity here, but there are other good things: the bridge over the River Tanat, the pub called 'The Horseshoe', with black and white frontage, and the architecturally fanciful schoolhouse. You will not regret, on a clear day, climbing above the village up the steep hill past the inn to enjoy the superb views, on the one hand into Wales and on the other towards the Shropshire plain, with the valleys of the Tanat and the Vyrnwy at your feet.

¶ The church, with its (almost) detached tower, is full of surprises, colour and texts; the work, originally, of a vicar with an exuberant imagination and immense energy. The memorial tablets repay study. Apparently those who came after the eccentric and artistic parson weren't all best pleased with what he had done. Fortunately for us, the parish undid their meddling in 1960, and restored the interior to the colourful state in which we see it now.

PLACES OF INTEREST IN THE NEIGHBOURHOOD

56. St. Winifred's Well (Woolston)

45. Old Oswestry (Oswestry)

FOOD AND ACCOMMODATION

Try the irresistible pub, but don't offend the fishermen, who are much in evidence in this delightful village. Plenty of places in Oswestry.

26 Built Fast but Built to Last

POSITION: Much Wenlock

ORDNANCE MAP: Landranger 138. Kidderminster & Wyre Forest.

MAP REF: SJ625000

ACCESS: In Wilmore Street, in the middle of Much Wenlock. You can't miss it!

NOTE: The Guildhall, a superb black-and-white building, was put up in two days by one Walter Hancock, (who also built Condover Hall and Shrewsbury's Old Market Hall) in 1577. It stands on oak posts over the butter market, which has also served as a prison. Upstairs is the panelled court-room and council chamber.
¶ The town shows evidence of fascinating history, when it was bigger and more important (but never more charming) than nowadays.

PLACES OF INTEREST IN THE NEIGHBOURHOOD
39. Wenlock Edge
19. Christ's Entry into Jerusalem (Aston Eyre)

FOOD AND ACCOMMODATION
The town can provide.

27 The Mystery of an Empire-builder's Grave

POSITION: Moreton Say

ORDNANCE MAP: Landranger 127. Stafford, Telford, etc.

MAP REF: SJ630345

ACCESS: The small settlement of Moreton Say is best approached by the unclassified road just north of Bletchley on the A41(T) about 8 miles east of Whitchurch.

NOTE: The interesting thing about the grave of Robert, Lord Clive is that nobody knows exactly where it is. Visitors have been spotted spending much time photographing a superior-looking monument in the churchyard, only to find that the Robert Clive it commemorates is not *the* Robert Clive but a Styche Hall worthy bearing the same name. The rector saves some from embarrassment; how many others return home with a photograph of the wrong memorial?

¶Most schoolboys, and all imperialists, will know that Robert, Lord Clive, a rascal at school, played a leading part in the conquest of India in the 18th century, and came home, rich and successful, to be MP for Shrewsbury.

¶Later, he was accused of corruption and impeached. He died in 1774, at his London home, of an overdose of laudanum. Was it an accident, or did he commit suicide while depressed? His family at Moreton Say had him buried in the church, at an unmarked spot. A memorial tablet on the south wall briefly records his achievements.

PLACES OF INTEREST IN THE NEIGHBOURHOOD

80. The Cast-iron Canal Aqueduct (Longdon-on-Tern)

FOOD AND ACCOMMODATION

Go to Whitchurch.

28 A Romantic Roofless Ruin

POSITION: Moreton Corbet

ORDNANCE MAP: Landranger 126. Shrewsbury, etc.

MAP REF: SJ5612231

ACCESS: From the substantial village of Shawbury seven miles north-east of Shrewsbury take the B5063 going due north for a mile or so, then look for a sign offering you Moreton Corbet along an unclassified road to your right.

NOTE: There will be no difficulty in recognising this splendid ruin. An unusual feature is that it occupies a flat, unprotected site. The dignified Elizabethan walls present a remarkable silhouette, which has been variously described as melodramatic, mournful and exciting. The ruins make the subject of a good photograph.
¶ The castle is now maintained by English Heritage, is open at all reasonable times, and there is no admission charge. Take your camera!

PLACES OF INTEREST IN THE NEIGHBOURHOOD
72. Grinshill Quarries (Grinshill)

FOOD AND ACCOMMODATION
Public house in Shawbury.
Shrewsbury.

29 The Maidens' Garlands

POSITION: Minsterley Church

ORDNANCE MAP: Landranger 126. Shrewsbury, etc.

MAP REF: SJ374050

ACCESS: In Minsterley village, on the left of the B4499 Worthen road, a short distance from its junction with the A488 Bishop's Castle road, 10 miles from Shrewsbury.

NOTE: There are maidens' garlands in several Shropshire rural churches, most of them with a sad story concerning a village virgin, usually engaged to a local swain, who met her death by accident or illness before the wedding could take place. Sometimes the girl died on the way to church, or immediately after the ceremony.
¶ Minsterley has no fewer than seven of these 'crants', as they are sometimes called, one in a protective showcase, and the other half-dozen hung up out of harm's way in transparent covers. Each consists, or consisted originally, of a linen-covered wooden frame decorated with flowers and gloves and streamers, all made of paper. These used to be placed beside the unfortunate girl's regular seat in the church.
¶ The astonishing thing is that some of these garlands should have lasted 200 years without crumbling into dust.

PLACES OF INTEREST IN THE NEIGHBOURHOOD
47. The Miners' Retreat (Snailbeach)
51. The Devil's Chair (Stiperstones)

FOOD AND ACCOMMODATION
Minsterley public-houses. Pontesbury has a restaurant and public-houses.

30 The Stone Circle at Mitchell's Fold

POSITION: On Stapeley Hill

ORDNANCE MAP: Landranger 137. Ludlow, Wenlock Edge etc.

MAP REF: SO303982

ACCESS: Turn right off the A488 Shrewsbury–Bishop's Castle road 16 miles from Shrewsbury (at approx. map ref. SO319179) on to an unclassified road which leads to The Marsh and on to Priest Weston and Chirbury. The road bends sharply right then left after one and a half miles; here is the signboard for Mitchell's Fold, and here you should leave your car while you walk the half-mile or so northwards along the track to the stone circle.

NOTE: On the often bleak and windy south-western slope of the hill are the remains of three Bronze Age stone circles, known as Mitchell's Fold, the Whetstones and Marsh Pool.
¶ One of the variants of the associated legend has it that during famine long ago a magic cow appeared, able to supply a pailful of milk to any needy local. Then one dark night a witch called Mitchell milked the cow into a pail with a sieve at the bottom. The puzzled beast let down her milk until a flash of lightning revealed to her that it was simply draining away into the ground. She bestowed a mighty kick upon the witch and ran off, never to be seen again.

PLACES OF INTEREST IN THE NEIGHBOURHOOD
35. An Unusual Church (Minsterley)
29. The Maidens' Garlands (Minsterley)
51. The Devil's Chair (Stiperstones)
47. The Miners' Retreat (Snailbeach)

FOOD AND ACCOMMODATION
Public-houses at Minsterley and Pontesbury.

31 The Pastoral Church

POSITION: Melverley

ORDNANCE MAP: Landranger 126. Shrewsbury, etc.

MAP REF: SJ333166

ACCESS: From the B4393, a quarter of a mile from Crew Green, cross the old railway bridge to the hamlet of Melverley in about 1½ miles. The church is at the end of a short road to your left.

NOTE: This is a quite unusual fifteenth-century black and white church, with a lot of robust oaken beams inside. There is an Elizabethan altar, a Saxon font, Jacobean furniture and a gallery. It is the best of only three half-timbered places of worship in the county, and the only one in regular use.

¶ The leaflet available in the chuch calls your attention to the facts that the timbers are pegged, not nailed, and that the Bible has been chained to the reading-desk since 1723.

¶ The setting of the church, above the river Vyrnwy, close to its confluence with the river Severn, is romantic and tranquil, protected by churchyard yews and surrounded by green meadows.

PLACES OF INTEREST IN THE NEIGHBOURHOOD

24. The Prince's Oak (Alberbury)
37. Old Parr (Wollaston)

FOOD AND ACCOMMODATION

There is an inn near the church.

32 The Bull Ring

POSITION: Loppington

ORDNANCE MAP: Landranger 126. Shrewsbury, etc.

MAP REF: SJ471293

ACCESS: From the winding A528 (Shrewsbury–Ellesmere) highway, drive east from Cockshutt through English Frankton for a convoluted 2½ miles or so, or north-east from Burlton village for the same sort of distance.

NOTE: It is claimed that this is the only genuine bull-baiting ring left in the county. It is secured in the roadway (after a substantial fall of rain, in a puddle) in front of the Dickin Arms.

¶ Bulls may have been baited in the same way as bears. The landlord of an inn could pay the bear-keeper ten shillings for three days' hire. The bear (or bull) was tethered to the ring; the keeper received two or three pence for three runs at the bear from each dog-owner. He usually had about him a piece of wood to lever open a dog's jaws when they fastened too tightly on the bear. The bear, or bull, could be baited three or four times a day, a collection being made each time. The keeper must have found this business quite lucrative.

¶ Loppington's last reported bear-baiting was in 1825, as part of a local wedding celebration. The vicar of the day put a stop to it. The bear-man, one Robinson, came from Hanmer.

PLACES OF INTEREST IN THE NEIGHBOURHOOD

38. Prince Moshueshue's Grave (Welshampton)
58. The Van Gogh Canal Bridge (Tilstock)

FOOD AND ACCOMMODATION

The Dickin Arms is only a step away from Northwood. Wem and Ellesmere are nearby.

33 Church Furniture of the Past

POSITION: St. Martin's

ORDNANCE MAP: Landranger 126. Shrewsbury, etc.

MAP REF: SJ323363

ACCESS: The church can easily be seen from the B5069, but is some little distance from the road. The key-holder lives in one of the attractive almshouses alongside the church.

NOTE: Until a few years ago the magnificent 3-tiered pulpit with its canopy and velvet fittings, and the box pews with their engraved brass plates, were still *in situ*. But the ravages of time were becoming apparent and urgent refurbishment of all the church furniture had to be put in hand.
¶ The pulpit has been re-erected at the back of the church and the brass plates have been put up in the chancel. A box pew is soon to be reassembled, for its curiosity value, beside the pulpit.

PLACES OF INTEREST IN THE NEIGHBOURHOOD
5. The Italian Station (Gobowen)
70. A Stonehenge Folly (Weston Rhyn)
6. A Venerable Churchyard Yew (Dudleston)

FOOD AND ACCOMMODATION
Village public-houses in the vicinity.

34 Where a Ruined Castle is a Monument to Treachery

POSITION: Hopton Castle

ORDNANCE MAP: Landranger 137. Ludlow, Wenlock Edge etc.

MAP REF: SO367779

ACCESS: Off the B4368 (Craven Arms–Clun) road at Purslow, go over the River Clun and turn off at Three Ashes for half a mile to Hopton Castle village. The ruinous keep is on a hump beyond two brooks, and you could easily get your feet wet jumping to it.

NOTE: In 1644, during the Civil War, the castle was owned by the Wallop family, who were loyal Parliamentarians. The Royalists laid siege to it. The defenders withstood artillery and undermining for three weeks, but at the end of that time agreed to surrender on condition that their lives were spared. Sadly, the attackers reneged on their agreement and slaughtered their gallant enemies, only the Governor being taken prisoner to Ludlow.

PLACES OF INTEREST IN THE NEIGHBOURHOOD
20. The Arbor Tree (Aston-on-Clun)
60. The Direction Pillar (Little Brampton)

FOOD AND ACCOMMODATION
At Craven Arms or Clun.

35 An Unusual Church

POSITION: Minsterley

ORDNANCE MAP: Landranger 126. Shrewsbury, etc.

MAP REF: SJ374050

ACCESS: See Curiosity No. 29.

NOTE: Minsterley church was built in the seventeenth century, a time when very few places of worship were being erected in Britain, by the Thynne family of Minsterley Hall. Besides being built largely of brick, it has odd architectural and decorative features (around door and windows) on the west frontage.

¶ Inside, the visitor's eye will be caught by the pulpit and tester, the gallery, font, communion-rail, and saloon-type doors to the chancel, all contemporary with the church.

PLACES OF INTEREST IN THE NEIGHBOURHOOD

47. The Miners' Retreat (Snailbeach)
51. The Devil's Chair (Stiperstones)

FOOD AND ACCOMMODATION

Village pubs at Minsterley, Pontesbury and Hanwood.

36 Langley Chapel

POSITION: Langley

ORDNANCE MAP: Landranger 126. Shrewsbury, etc.

MAP REF: SJ537001

ACCESS: The chapel is best approached from Acton Burnell, which is seven miles south of Shrewsbury, and reached via an unclassified road network and accurate reading of the OS map. From Acton Burnell drive south a further mile and a half, then first turn left, in the direction of Hughley and Kenley, and look for the familiar English Heritage sign on your right after about a quarter of a mile.

NOTE: The attraction of the chapel, which is in a field (liberally manured when we were there last) is the Jacobean furnishings and fittings, which are rarely found nowadays. These survived because after the seventeenth century the building wasn't much used. The positions of the reading-desk and altar should be noted. Look upwards at the interesting ceiling, and then observe the seating arrangements—you sat then not where you fancied, but in a place deemed appropriate to your social standing.

PLACES OF INTEREST IN THE NEIGHBOURHOOD
73. The Burnell Burnished Brass (Acton Burnell)
13. A Modest Telford Bridge (Cantlop)
71. The Condover Memorials (Condover)

FOOD AND ACCOMMODATION
Make your way to Much Wenlock.

37 Old Parr

POSITION: Wollaston.

ORDNANCE MAP: Landranger 126. Shrewsbury, etc.

MAP REF: SJ329123

ACCESS: The hamlet of Wollaston is just off the A458(T) Shrewsbury–Welshpool road, about ten miles from Shrewsbury. The key to the church is available from the nearby farm.

NOTE: Old Parr is reputed to have lived to be nearly 153. He was a farm worker whose diet consisted of 'rancid cheese, milk, coarse hard bread, and small drink, usually whey'. The story goes that the King wanted to see this remarkable fellow. Not surprisingly, the long journey to London proved too much for him. But his was the rare distinction of burial in Westminster Abbey.
¶Parr was distinguished not only by his longevity, but also by his virility. He is said to have married at 80, and fathered two children, then taken a second wife when he was 120, and fathered a third child. There are even sly stories about his extra-marital activities.
¶None of this is authenticated and some suggest there were two Thomas Parrs, father and son—at any rate, a tablet in the church tells you all about him.

PLACES OF INTEREST IN THE NEIGHBOURHOOD
24. The Prince's Oak (Alberbury)
35. An Unusual Church (Minsterley)

FOOD AND ACCOMMODATION IN THE NEIGHBOURHOOD
Middletown, Halfway House, Westbury, Welshpool.

38 Prince Moshueshue's Grave

POSITION: Welshampton

ORDNANCE MAP: Landranger 126. Shrewsbury, etc.

MAP REF: SJ433349

ACCESS: Welshampton church is alongside the A495 road between Ellesmere and Whitchurch, about four and a half miles from the former town. The vertical gravestone is on the right-hand side of the path as you approach the church from the gate.

NOTE: This is an unusual memorial to find in a village churchyard in rural Shropshire, for Moshueshue was the son of an African chief. We are told that his full name was Jeremiah Lebopena Moshueshue, and that his father was King of the Basutos, in South Africa.

¶A surprisingly unpretentious gravestone it is, not a lot different from the other stones which mark the graves of villagers who were buried in the same part of the yard around that time.

¶Prince Moshueshue died aged 23 on August 26th 1863, the epitaph tells us. He was at that time a student of St. Augustine's Missionary College.

PLACES OF INTEREST IN THE NEIGHBOURHOOD

40. The Church made Famous by a Shropshire Chronicler (Myddle)
32. The Bull Ring (Loppington)

FOOD AND ACCOMMODATION

At Ellesmere or Shrewsbury.

39 Wenlock Edge

POSITION: Running roughly south-west to north-east for 15 miles betwen Craven Arms and Much Wenlock.

ORDNANCE MAP: Landranger 137. Ludlow, Wenlock Edge etc.

ACCESS: Easily approachable from either end—and several intermediate points, including Church Stretton. There is a car park, together with a picnic site and nature trail, at SO4798767, for footsloggers.

NOTE: Wenlock Edge has been described as the best example of an escarpment in Britain—that is, a ridge with a steep face on one side and a gentle drop-slope on the other. Housman drew attention to its dominance as a feature of the south-west Shropshire landscape with the verse begining 'On Wenlock Edge the wood's in trouble'. The National Trust has bought great stretches of it and develops and maintains the network of footpaths.

¶For a long time now limestone has been quarried from the ridge, and a tramway was used, until 1952, to take it down to the kilns at Harley Bank.

¶To-day's sightseers, picnickers, motorists and ramblers use the B4371 road along the Edge and the woodland paths to enjoy the lovely views over Corvedale, Ape Dale and Hope Dale, peaceful valleys with enchanting, scattered villages. The best viewing point might be Ippikin's Rock (SO592989), or at SO573968, a quarter of a mile or so to the south-west.

¶At Major's Leap (SO592989) the Royalist Major Smallman is said to have jumped off on horseback to escape his pursuers during the Civil War.

PLACES OF INTEREST IN THE NEIGHBOURHOOD

26. Built Fast, but Built to Last (Much Wenlock)
49. The Rude Lady (Holdgate)

FOOD AND ACCOMMODATION

At Much Wenlock or Craven Arms.

40 The Church made Famous by a Shropshire Chronicler

POSITION: Myddle

ORDNANCE MAP: Landranger 126. Shrewsbury, etc.

MAP REF: SJ467236

ACCESS: Myddle village lies alongside an unclassified road off the A528 between Shrewsbury and Ellesmere. It is seven miles north-north-west of the county town.

NOTE: Those who have read Richard Gough's *History of Myddle* will recall how this observant and well-respected local farmer compiled his unique record of his contemporaries, moving methodically through the village families with their permanent church seating as a guide, so that he left no-one out.

¶His notes are sometimes scurrilous, often humorous, and from his observations we are able to obtain valuable information about the local history, conventions and gossip of a typical English village community at the very end of the seventeenth century.

¶Don't miss the ducking-stool, minus the pole, hanging on the wall, nor the sorry remains of Robin Hood Kynaston's castle close at hand.

PLACES OF INTEREST IN THE NEIGHBOURHOOD

32. The Bull Ring (Loppington)
38. Prince Moshueshue's Grave (Welshampton)

FOOD AND ACCOMMODATION

One of the Myddle pubs, or Ellesmere, or Shrewsbury.

41 The Highwayman who Lived with Beelzebub in a Cave

POSITION: Nesscliffe

ORDNANCE MAP: Landranger 126. Shrewsbury, etc.

MAP REF: SJ386192

ACCESS: Nesscliffe village lies on Telford's A5(T) road between Shrewsbury and Oswestry, eight miles from the first, ten miles from the latter. Kynaston's Cave and the 26 steps leading up to it are on the main road side of Nesscliffe Hill, which is the sandstone outcrop, spiked with conifers, opposite the Three Pigeons hostelry.

NOTE: Humphrey Kynaston had a good job at Myddle Castle until he killed a man and was outlawed. He then made his home in this Nesscliffe cave—which others, before and after his time, also found habitable. This was at the beginning of the sixteenth century, when there was a regular passage of rich wool merchants linking the Welsh sheep-farmers who visited Oswestry market with the town of Shrewsbury.

¶Kynaston adopted the life of a Shropshire Robin Hood, raiding the wealthy to succour the poor, who not surprisingly approved of this system, and kept Wild Humphrey and his horse Beelzebub provisioned and well-informed. When the crafty sheriff removed planks from Montford Bridge and laid an ambush to catch the outlaw, he set his horse to leap the 29-foot gap and escaped. For many years afterwards there were markers in a nearby field to demonstrate to disbelievers the extent of this prodigious jump.

PLACES OF INTEREST IN THE NEIGHBOURHOOD

56. St. Winifred's Well (Wollaston)

31. The Pastoral Church (Melverley)

FOOD AND ACCOMMODATON

There are some inviting-looking public-houses in the villages along this road.

42 A Modern Black-and-White Church

POSITION: All Saints' Church, Little Stretton

ORDNANCE MAP: Landranger 137. Ludlow, Wenlock Edge etc.

MAP REF: SO444919

ACCESS: Turn off the A49 one and a half miles south of Church Stretton for Little Stretton. The church is beside the road through the village.

NOTE: This delightful building may be disregarded by many writers of guidebooks because it is not very old. It is thatched, has a black-and-white exterior, and is panelled inside entirely with pitchpine. It is set about with lawns and flower-beds and looks attractive and serene.

¶There is a notice inside which tells you that one Alice Elizabeth Gibbon was responsible for its building in 1903, and a remarkable eulogy describing her life and work in the village. She died in 1932.

PLACES OF INTEREST IN THE NEIGHBOURHOOD

1. Flounder's Folly (Culmington)
57. Always on a Thursday (Church Stretton)

FOOD AND ACCOMMODATION

Several restaurants in Church Stretton.

43 The Old Butter Cross

POSITION: Newport

ORDNANCE MAP: Landranger 127. Stafford, Telford, etc.

MAP REF: SJ745192

ACCESS: Next to St. Nicholas' Church, in the High Street.

NOTE: The Old Butter Cross is a stone shaft on a plinth. It is believed that the cross it supported, long gone, was a casualty of the Civil War, broken off by some of Cromwell's men.

¶ Originally the cross was erected to the memory of one Sir Roger de Puleston, who fought for King Edward I. He was rewarded by being made Sheriff of Anglesey but was killed not long afterwards. Sir Roger's home was at Puleston, just north of Newport.

¶ The name Butter Cross derives from the butter market, where the monument was housed, and it was given protection with railings when that building was knocked down. Since then it has been re-sited more than once, but it has kept its name.

PLACES OF INTEREST IN THE NEIGHBOURHOOD

7. The Matthew Webb Monument (Dawley)
79. The Mary Tooth Tomb (Madeley)

FOOD AND ACCOMMODATION

A sufficiency in Newport.

44 New St. Chad's

POSITION: In Shrewsbury, overlooking the Quarry park.

ORDNANCE MAP: Landranger 137. Ludlow, Wenlock Edge etc.

MAP REF: SJ487130

ACCESS: From the town centre, look for the cross on the dome.

NOTE: 'New' because it replaced Old St. Chad's. But it was built almost exactly 200 years ago. It is said to be England's largest round church. In fact, it consists of two intersecting circles, with a good staircase curving up from the smaller of them to the gallery in the circular nave.

¶ At the west end, above the portico and vestries, is a square tower, then an octagonal section. Above that is a circular stage with columns, topped by a dome with a gilded cross.

¶ The choir has sung on occasions of national rejoicing from the tower gallery. More frequently, the excellent 12-bell ring of bells is heard over the town and the river-girt Quarry park opposite.

¶ The church, always a cause for dispute between those who approve its design and those who find it deplorable, was built by Steuart on the site of part of the medieval town walls.

PLACES OF INTEREST IN THE NEIGHBOURHOOD

63. Sabrina and the Shoemakers' Arbor (Shrewsbury)
50. Grope Lane (Shrewsbury)
75. The Refectory Pulpit (Shrewsbury)
62. The Column (Shrewsbury)

FOOD AND ACCOMMODATION

Ample in the town.

45 Old Oswestry

POSITION: Just north of Oswestry.

ORDNANCE MAP: Landranger 137. Ludlow, Wenlock Edge etc.

MAP REF: SJ295310

ACCESS: Near the old road between Oswestry and Gobowen. It's easy to see. A reasonable track leads from the road to the town end of the hillock, as it were, and, from the town suburbs, Llwyn Road towards Hengoed.

NOTE: This remarkable Iron Age hill fort dates from 700 B.C. It is an elaborate and extensive series of concentric ramparts and ditches, and was probably occupied by successive prehistoric tribes until the Romans came.

¶ You can imagine the central area with pit dwellings, then wooden huts, and finally stone-built houses, defended by earthworks to present a formidable defensive system. The whole site, called in Welsh Hen Dinan, has been estimated to have covered as much as 56 acres. Note the way the earthworks follow the contours of the hill, the position of the gateways, and the wide views from the top of the mounds.

PLACES OF INTEREST IN THE NEIGHBOURHOOD

5. The Italian Station (Gobowen)
9. Four Ways to Cross a Valley (Chirk)
70. A Stonehenge Folly (Weston Rhyn)
78. Oswald's Well (Oswestry)

FOOD AND ACCOMMODATION

Ample in Oswestry.

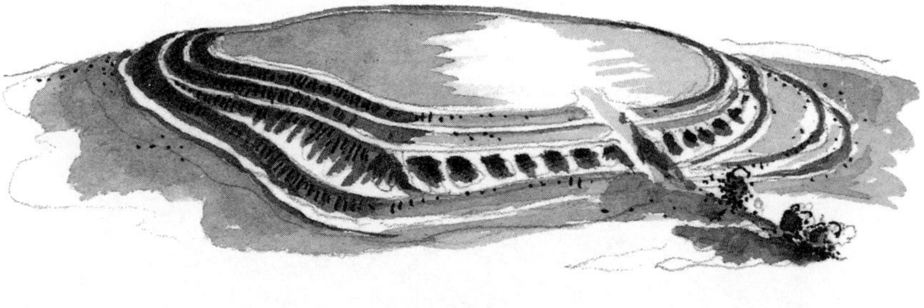

46 The Drunken Steeplejack

POSITION: St. Alkmund's Church, Shrewsbury

ORDNANCE MAP: Landranger 126. Shrewsbury, etc.

ACCESS: Entry from Fish Street.

NOTE: Oddly, St. Alkmund's and St. Julian's stand cheek by jowl, with St. Mary's just around the corner. When St. Alkmund's was taken down and rebuilt after 1788, following the alarming collapse of old St. Chad's, the tower and spire were left *in situ*. On top of the spire is one of the 'vanes of Shrewsbury', which, according to the poet Housman, 'gleam Islanded in Severn stream'.

¶ In 1584 a 'simple, lame fellow' called George Archer climbed the spire on four separate occasions 'with clouted shoes upon his feet', so presumably without benefit of ladders or scaffolding. The first time he brought down the weathercock, which was 27 inches from beak to tail and weighed 12 lbs. A week later he replaced it, on that occasion entertaining the fast-assembling spectators below by dancing a jig on the bar supporting the cross.

¶ The next time he climbed the spire he attracted attention and applause by taking up with him a drum and a bow, with arrows. At the top he beat the drum and, perhaps to justify his name, shot an arrow into the air. On his final climb he caused the cockerel to revolve, and danced, hooted and shouted for nearly two hours.

¶ He fared better than poor Cadman at St. Mary's (64), returning safely to terra firma on each occasion. The secret of Archer's success may have lain in his always being drunk when he clambered up but sober when he came down again.

PLACES OF INTEREST IN THE NEIGHBOURHOOD

55. Laura's Tower (Shrewsbury)
44. New St. Chad (Shrewsbury)
50. Grope Lane (Shrewsbury)

FOOD AND ACCOMMODATION

Plentiful in the town nowadays.

47 The Miners' Retreat

POSITION: Snailbeach

ORDNANCE MAP: Landranger 126. Shrewsbury, etc.

MAP REF: SJ374021

ACCESS: The Bishop's Castle road from Shrewsbury (A488) will take you direct through Pontesbury and Minsterley to Ploxgreen in about 10 miles. There, go left. You soon reach Snailbeach.

NOTE: There is evidence all around, as you climb into the Stiperstones region, of the mining activity which began with the Romans and came to a rather abrupt end about a hundred years ago. In this district were found rich deposits of lead and barytes, and useful amounts of several other metals, including silver.

¶What you see now are relics of the once thriving industry—glistening spoil heaps, crumbling ruins of engine-houses, vestiges of the mineral railway which once took the ore down to Minsterley and beyound. If you do some exploring, watch out for potholes and old and dangerous mineshafts!

¶The Stiperstones to the south is a popular summer haunt for walkers and, of course, industrial archeologists. A surprising number of people who enjoy living in this strangely attractive setting have created comfortable homes in the scattered hamlets up here. Evocative place-names in the district include Hope, Gavels, Shelve, and The Bog.

PLACES OF INTEREST IN THE NEIGHBOURHOOD

51. The Devil's Chair (Stiperstones)
35. An Unusual Church (Minsterley Church)
29. The Maidens' Garlands (Minsterley)

FOOD AND ACCOMMODATION

Not a bad place for a picnic, with some good views. There's a public-house up there as well.

48 The Bradling Stone

POSITION: On the village green at Norton-in-Hales.

ORDNANCE MAP: Landranger 127. Stafford, Telford, etc.

MAP REF: SJ703387

ACCESS: Take the A53 (Newcastle-under-Lyme) road from Market Drayton, then, two miles out, the B5415, left-handed. After two miles, there is a minor road of just over a mile into the village.

NOTE: The flattish-topped boulder has at least three stories explaining its place in the history of the village. The best-known one is that people caught working after midday on Shrove Tueday were bumped on the stone.

¶The second legend is that the rock was a boundary marker. Whenever the parish bounds were beaten, the youngsters were bumped on it to ensure that they remembered where the boundaries were. The third and most plausible theory is that years ago travelling gangs of farmworkers, having slaked their thirst at the nearby public-house, set up fights with each other, and placed their stake-money on the stone.

PLACES OF INTEREST IN THE NEIGHBOURHOOD

27. The Mystery of an Empire-builder's Grave (Moreton Say)
28. A Romantic, Roofless Ruin (Moreton Corbet)

FOOD AND ACCOMMODATION

Market Drayton, Moreton Say.

49 The Rude Lady

POSITION: Holdgate

ORDNANCE MAP: Landranger 137. Ludlow, Wenlock Edge etc.

MAP REF: SO561896

ACCESS: From the B4368 running through Corvedale, you should pick out the lane at Shipton leading south towards Stanton Long. Here, after driving into the village, you turn right-handed. You reach Holdgate in a mile or so. You climb a few steps to reach a quite dignified little Norman church.

NOTE: The sculpted sheila-na-gig, on the outside of the south wall of the church, is high up and quite small. It is probably the best of the four examples in Shropshire, being less weathered than the others.

¶A sheila-na-gig is a fertility figure and represents a female in a rather indelicate posture. Our forefathers were perhaps less prudish about these things than us.

¶Inside the church is a beautiful Norman font with elaborate carving. It may not be up to the high standard of the font at Stottesdon, but is most attractive, especially in sunlight and decked with flowers.

PLACES OF INTEREST IN THE NEIGHBOURHOOD

1. Flounder's Folly (Culmington)
39. Wenlock Edge

FOOD AND ACCOMMODATION

At Much Wenlock or Craven Arms.

50 Grope Lane

POSITION: In Shrewsbury

ORDNANCE MAP: Landranger 126. Shrewsbury, etc.

ACCESS: Off High Street, almost opposite the Square.

NOTE: A town guide may suggest to you that the name connotes the night-walker in the narrow, at one time unlighted passage, feeling his way along with outstretched arms to touch both walls at the same time. You could meet with those who put forward a less delicate explanation of the name.

¶ Shrewsbury is well-blessed, like other Tudor towns, with pedestrian thoroughfares, for which a local name is 'shuts'. Of these Grope Lane, with its overhanging timbers, and the first floors of the houses almost meeting overhead, is probably the finest, the most-used, and certainly the best-known. It leads up to Bear Steps, restored a few years ago by the local Civic Society.

PLACES OF INTEREST IN THE NEIGHBOURHOOD.

64. Where a Stuntman had a Great Fall (Shrewsbury)
46. The Drunken Steeplejack (Shrewsbury)
55. Laura's Tower (Shrewsbury)

FOOD AND ACCOMMODATION

One is spoilt for choice in Shrewsbury.

51 The Devil's Chair

POSITION: The Stiperstones

ORDNANCE MAP: Landranger 137. Ludlow, Wenlock Edge etc.

MAP REF: SO368992

ACCESS: From the A488 road from Shrewsbury to Bishop's Castle, look for the unclassified road just beyond Minsterley, at Ploxgreen, directing you to the Stiperstones. This has to be followed until you reach Pennerley. A further two miles or so along the road to Bridges there is a rudimentary but free car park (map ref. SO370977). From here a path leads up a rock-strewn slope to the sinister-looking Devil's Chair, one of a series of rocky outcrops along the ridge.

NOTE: This area is so wind-swept and aloof, especially in bad weather, that one is not surprised to learn that legends are associated with it.
1. The Devil came this way once, his apron full of stones. For some reason he dropped this load and left it here.
2. It is also said that the Shropshire coven of witches used to meet here under the chairmanship of the Old Tempter, and that when mist shrouds the 'Chair', there's mischief afoot.
3. Wild Edric, a local Saxon nobleman outlawed by William the Conqueror, used the Stiperstones as his stamping-ground. Sometimes he and his followers can be heard working in the derelict lead-mines which dot the side of the Stiperstones.
¶If you have doubts about the authenticity of these stories, you could enjoy the freshness of the air up here, and the views westward over the Clun Forest, the Long Mountain, Corndon Hill, the Berwyns and the Breiddens and eastward to the Long Mynd.

PLACES OF INTEREST IN THE NEIGHBOURHOOD.
47. The Miners' Retreat
35. An Unusual Church (Minsterley)
29. The Maidens' Garlands (Minsterley)

FOOD AND ACCOMMODATION
At Minsterley or Pontesbury.

52 The One-armed Clock

POSITION: Lydbury North

ORDNANCE MAP: Landranger 137. Ludlow, Wenlock Edge etc.

MAP REF: SO352861

NOTE: The church clock, with a clean, bold face on an even bolder tower, has only one arm, or hand. It dates back to the reign of Elizabeth I, to a time when one-armed clocks were commonplace. There is no way of fitting a minute hand to it, since its mechanism predates the invention of this part of the movement. It was built by Thomas Vernon of Ludlow, installed at Lydbury in 1728, and restored by an expert in 1973.
¶ While you are at the church, which is light and airy, with shining woodwork, notice a further three curiosities. One is the Roman Catholic chapel in the north transept, a rare feature in an Anglican church. Over the south transept is what used to be a schoolroom, but is now a store. The third is the rare wooden Laudian candlestick on either side of the altar. (See no. 69)

PLACES OF INTEREST IN THE NEIGHBOURHOOD
60. The Direction Pillar (Little Brampton)
20. The Arbor Tree (Aston-on-Clun)

FOOD AND ACCOMMODATION
Craven Arms or Clun.

53 The Face at The Feathers

POSITION: Ludlow

ORDNANCE MAP: Landranger 137. Ludlow, Wenlock Edge etc.

MAP REF: SO513753

ACCESS: Drive through Ludlow and you can hardly miss it. The Feathers Hotel is in the Bull Ring, and is a building of rare beauty and distinction.

NOTE: The wood-carving of the frontage is superb. Originally a private house, it was built right at the beginning of the seventeenth century, and the woodworkers must have had a field-day producing such exquisite work.

¶ Whose is the larger of the two faces in our picture? The man who commissioned the work? The master-carver himself? Probably, as in the case of church gargoyles, craftsmen used mates with unusual faces as models.

PLACES OF INTEREST IN THE NEIGHBOURHOOD

54. The Hexagonal Porch (Ludlow)
76. Where the Shropshire Lad at last found Peace (Ludlow)

FOOD AND ACCOMMODATION

Close at hand here.

54 The Hexagonal Porch

POSITION: St. Laurence's Church, Ludlow

ORDNANCE MAP: Landranger 137. Ludlow, Wenlock Edge etc.

MAP REF: SO520755

ACCESS: This huge parish church is hemmed in by other buildings, but its tower is a landmark for miles around.

NOTE: While many other churches have beautifully-carved misericords and similar treasures, very few have a six-sided porch. St. Laurence's shares this curious feature with another outstanding parish church, St. Mary Redcliffe, in Bristol.

¶The porch has two storeys, the upper having served as a school at one time. When you've passed through the porch, do not miss the choir stalls and the medieval stained glass.

PLACES OF INTEREST IN THE NEIGHBOURHOOD

76. Where the Shropshire Lad at last found Peace (Ludlow)
53. The Face at The Feathers

FOOD AND ACCOMMODATION

Adequate in the town.

55 Laura's Tower

POSITION: Shrewsbury, in the castle precincts in Castle Street.

ORDNANCE MAP: Landranger 126. Shrewsbury, etc.

ACCESS: The tower is prominent at the top of the slope on your right as you enter the castle grounds.

NOTE: The tower is a little-regarded folly, built by the busy Thomas Telford in 1787. He was brought to Shrewsbury by his countryman William Pulteney, M.P. for the Borough at the time, to convert the castle into a private residence. In the following year Telford became the county surveyor, which post he held until he died in 1834, and many and varied were the civil engineering projects which he successively and successfully undertook in that time.

¶The folly was built for Pulteney's wife. The tower where she perhaps sat on summer afternoons affords a panoramic view of the Severn, and the suburban landscape which now lies beyond the railway lines. Test your local history by imagining the scene which would have met Laura's gaze!

PLACES OF INTEREST IN THE NEIGHBOURHOOD

64. Where a Stuntman had a Great Fall (Shrewsbury)
46. The Drunken Steeplejack (Shrewsbury)
66. The Jesse Window

FOOD AND ACCOMMODATION

A variety of places to choose from in the town.

56 St. Winifred's Well

POSITION: The hamlet of Woolston, part of West Felton.

ORDNANCE MAP: Landranger 126. Shrewsbury, etc.

MAP REF: SJ323224

ACCESS: From West Felton on the A5(T) road, four miles south-east of Oswestry, take the minor road signposted Maesbury. At Woolston, immediately beyond the farm on the right, (The Laurels), look for double pedestrian gates protecting entry to a grassy lane. The well is below and beyond a tiny black-and-white dwelling surrounded by a clump of trees a few hundred yards along the lane.

NOTE: According to legend Winifred was the heart's desire of Caradoc, the son of a chief. But she wanted to dedicate her life to the church. Caradoc's attempt to force his attentions upon her led to her violent death. Where she fell a spring of water appeared.

¶Her body was brought from Holywell, the scene of the crime, to Shrewsbury. One of the places where her bearers rested was Woolston, and here another spring of pure water appeared. An entertaining account of these happenings can be found in Ellis Peters' novel *A Morbid Taste for Bones*.

¶The water rises in a recess, with a cross set in the floor, and overflows into two stone basins, approached by steps on either side. It was deemed to have curative properties, especially for eye complaints.

¶At one time, not so long ago, the spring provided an unfailing supply of pure water for the hamlet.

PLACES OF INTEREST IN THE NEIGHBOURHOOD

45. Old Oswestry (Oswestry)
5. The Italian Station (Gobowen)

FOOD AND ACCOMMODATION

Ample in Oswestry.

57 Always on a Thursday

POSITION: Church Stretton

ORDNANCE MAP: Landranger 137. Ludlow, Wenlock Edge etc.

MAP REF: SO452957

ACCESS: Leave the A49 at the traffic lights and proceed up Sandford Avenue. Turn left into High Street for the church and a car park.

NOTE: The gravestone of Ann Cook, who died in 1814, and was buried in this churchyard, is on the south side of the church. It is sometimes called the Thursday tomb, though it's not really a tomb. The epitaph reads:

On a Thursday she was born
On a Thursday made a bride
On a Thursday her leg was broke
And on a Thursday she died.

¶ On the outside of this church is one of Shropshire's sheila-na-gigs. (If you're not sure what this is, see no. 49.) The one here, above the door, is so badly weathered that the pure-minded Arthur Mee described the figure as a 'little old man'. Inside the church is a piscina, high on a window-sill, so positioned because it belonged to the altar on a former rood-loft.

PLACES OF INTEREST IN THE NEIGHBOURHOOD

1. Flounder's Folly (Culmington)
42. A Modern Black-and-White Church (Little Stretton)
39. Wenlock Edge

FOOD AND ACCOMMODATION

In Church Stretton.

58 A Van Gogh Canal Bridge

POSITION: On Whixall Moss, near Tilstock

ORDNANCE MAP: Landranger 126. Shrewsbury, etc.

MAP REF: SJ517378

ACCESS: Hard to find! From the A41(T) (Shrewsbury) road two and a quarter miles south of Whitchurch, take the minor road, on the right, signposted Tilstock. At Tilstock cross the B5476, making for Fenn's Wood. After two miles of narrow lane go right, and shortly left, to the bridge, which you should be able to see, the land being Fenland flat hereabouts.

NOTE: The counterweighted bridge is one of a group of three on the Llangollen Canal in the Tilstock area. The platform can be raised to an angle of 45 degress to allow boats to pass. The older bridges of this type are opened by pulling on a chain, not entirely without hazard. On one occasion a platform was blown back and killed someone on a boat passing beneath the structure. Since that time the mechanism has been replaced by a hydraulically-operated type, controlled by a windlass.

PLACES OF INTEREST IN THE NEIGHBOURHOOD

2. A Superb Norman Doorway
21. The Heart of the 'Scourge of France'
72. Grinshill Quarries

FOOD AND ACCOMMODATION

Calverhall and a couple of restaurants in Whitchurch.

59 A Quiet Church in a Quiet Town

POSITION: Clun

ORDNANCE MAP: Landranger 137. Ludlow, Wenlock Edge etc.

MAP REF: SO301805

ACCESS: At the top of Church Street.

NOTE: This solid little church has several unusual features. It is approached by steps through a most attractive lychgate, where a coffin and its bearers could be sheltered from the rain. There is a pyramid roof to the typically robust border tower, and a former schoolroom over the porch.

¶ The rarest feature, inside the church, is an old canopy from which, in medieval times, the host, the consecrated wafer of the Eucharist, would have been hung.

PLACES OF INTEREST IN THE NEIGHBOURHOOD

60. The Direction Pillar (Little Brampton)
52. The One-armed Clock (Lydbury North)

FOOD AND ACCOMMODATION

There is a restaurant in the town.

60 The Direction Pillar

POSITION: At the cross-roads at Little Brampton.

ORDNANCE MAP: Landranger 137. Ludlow, Wenlock Edge etc.

MAP REF: SO368814

ACCESS: Beside the B4368, about halfway between Craven Arms and Clun.

NOTE: This unusual stone and metal finger-post carries at its foot a plate which says it all:
'This Direction Pillar was erected in 1800 by the Second Lord Clive afterwards created first earl of Powis and taken down, removed and renovated during the road improvements in 1929.'
¶Situated among Housman's 'quietest places under the sun', it points the way to Ludlow, C. Gunford (Clungunford), B. (Bishops) Castle, and Clun, these names being stencilled in capital letters through the metal arms.

PLACES OF INTEREST IN THE NEIGHBOURHOOD
20. The Arbor Tree
52. The One-armed Clock (Lydbury North)
59. A Quiet Church in a Quiet Town (Clun)

FOOD AND ACCOMMODATION
Craven Arms: hotel and restaurant.
Clun.

61 The Paintings on the Wall

POSITION: Claverley

ORDNANCE MAP: Landranger 138. Kidderminster & Wyre Forest.

MAP REF: SO 793935

ACCESS: All Saints' Church is at the centre of the village of Claverley, seven and a half miles east of Bridgnorth, and signposted from several points from the A454 or the A458 along unclassified roads.

NOTE: The frieze, dating from the early thirteenth century, and at first sight similar in style to the Bayeux Tapestry, was uncovered during restoration work in 1902. It depicts fifteen horsemen in battle, and is thought to represent the conflict between Christian virtue and pagan vice.

¶ The church contains several other curiosities, including two very early stone fonts, the alabaster tomb, dated 1558, of lawyer Sir Richard Brooke, with his two wives and 17 children, and, in the north-west corner, a clock movement which, the notice hazards, could be the only one of its type in the British Isles.

PLACES OF INTEREST IN THE NEIGHBOURHOOD

15. The Tipsy Tower (Bridgnorth)
17. The Cliff Railway (Bridgnorth)

FOOD AND ACCOMMODATION

Available at Claverley.

62 The Column

POSITION: Shrewsbury

ORDNANCE MAP: Landranger 126. Shrewsbury, etc.

MAP REF: SJ507121

ACCESS: There should be no difficulty in finding this huge structure, at the roundabout outside the Shirehall at the east end of Abbey Foregate.

NOTE: Any guidebook will tell you that at 133 feet 6 inches, this is the tallest Doric column in the world.
¶ The fluted column, with its crowning statue, commemorates the first Viscount Hill, a locally born soldier who distinguished himself in Egypt, in the Peninsular Wars and at Waterloo, and who rose to be Commander-in-Chief of the British Army (1828).
¶ A steep spiral staircase of 172 steps within the Column leads up to a railed balcony near the top, which gives magnificent all-round views over Shrewsbury and environs. The key to the entrance is available from the Shirehall, and you may be called upon to make a deposit to help you to remember to return it.

PLACES OF INTEREST IN THE NEIGHBOURHOOD
75. The Refectory Pulpit (Shrewsbury)
44. New St. Chad's (Shrewsbury)
50. Grope Lane (Shrewsbury)

FOOD AND ACCOMMODATION
Freely available in Shrewsbury.

63 Sabrina and the Shoemakers' Arbour

POSITION: Shrewsbury

ORDNANCE MAP: Landranger 126. Shrewsbury, etc.

ACCESS: In the Dingle in Quarry Park, overlooking the pool.

NOTE: The recently re-sited figure of Sabrina and the Shoemakers' Guild Arbour are attractive features of the Dingle gardens, on the site of the quarry from which the park takes its name. The whole complex is associated with the generous Shropshire Horticultural Society committee, among whose past officials was the late Percy Thrower.

¶ According to legend, Sabrina is the goddess of the nearby Severn, and arose from its waters. Her story formed part of Milton's 'Comus' when it was staged at Ludlow Castle.

¶ The arbour is a tribute to the trade guilds, which in more rumbustious times than these took part in an annual knees-up on public land over and above the curve of the river at Kingsland. But these jollifications became so much of an undisciplined rough-and-tumble, stimulated by excessive drink, that the corporation put its foot down. The much more sedate (but nationally renowned) Floral Fête developed into to-day's August Flower Show.

PLACES OF INTEREST IN THE NEIGHBOURHOOD

44. New St. Chad's (Shrewsbury)
62. The Column (Shrewsbury)
75. The Refectory Pulpit (Shrewsbury)

FOOD AND ACCOMMODATION

A good selection in the town.

64 Where a Stuntman had a Great Fall

POSITION: Shrewsbury.

ORDNANCE MAP: Landranger 126. Shrewsbury, etc.

ACCESS: In St. Mary's Street, off the higher end of the Pride Hill pedestrian precinct.

NOTE: Direct your gaze upwards from the relative safety of the pavement and look at the spire of St. Mary's Church. (The spire, together with that of St. Alkmund's, standing on the highest points of the town within the river loop, can be seen to best advantage from Coleham Head, over the English Bridge, or Luciefelde Road, off Longden Road.)

¶ Some writers claim that St. Mary's has the third highest spire in England, after Salisbury and Norwich cathedrals. It was built towards the end of the fifteenth century, on a lowish tower, so its overall height from the ground is unremarkable.

¶ Forever associated with St. Mary's spire is the name of Robert Cadman, a 28-year-old stuntman, who proposed to 'fly', on a frosty day in 1739, along a rope secured from the top of the spire, around which there was repair scaffolding, to a point on the other side of the river. He is reported to have attached a pair of 'wings' to his body, and he intended to walk or slide down the rope while his common-law wife jingled a collecting-box under the upturned noses of a considerable crowd gathered between the church and the river to watch the feat. However, things went wrong, the young man fell off the rope and was killed. A plaque on the wall of the church carries a verse commemorating the incident.

PLACES OF INTEREST IN THE NEIGHBOURHOOD

46. The Drunken Steeplejack (Shrewsbury)
66. The Jesse Window (Shrewsbury)
55. Laura's Tower (Shrewsbury)
50. Grope Lane (Shrewsbury)

FOOD AND ACCOMMODATION

Ample in the town.

65 Public Punishment Devices

POSITION: Norton

ORDNANCE MAP: Landranger 127. Stafford, Telford, etc.

MAP REF: SJ728004

NOTE: The stocks and whipping-post are beside the busy A442 Telford–Bridgnorth road just over five miles north of the latter town, on a small patch of green in front of the church.

¶ There are not many of these public punishment devices on view, outside museums. In medieval times the heavy frame was used, often in the market-place where fairs were held, to secure delinquents by the ankles and expose them to public ridicule and shame. Persons so immobilised would have made a (literally) sitting target for rotting fruit and other offensive matter.

¶ The whipping-post, for thieves and other felons, must have been even more painful and degrading.

PLACES OF INTEREST IN THE NEIGHBOURHOOD

7. The Matthew Webb Monument (Dawley)
79. The Mary Tooth Tomb (Madeley)
17. The Cliff Railway (Bridgnorth)

FOOD AND ACCOMMODATION

At Bridgnorth or in Telford.

66 The Jesse Window

POSITION: Shrewsbury

ORDNANCE MAP: Landranger 126. Shrewsbury, etc.

ACCESS: In St. Mary's church, in St. Mary's Street, and not at all difficult to find.

NOTE: The most striking feature of the many assorted good things in this now redundant church is the glass, most of which has come from other places of worship.

¶ Much came from Germany: that from the north aisle from Trier, some windows from a Cistercian Abbey near Cologne, and other glass from a nunnery in the Rhineland. Yet more came from the Belgian town of Liège. The glass in the north aisle came from Trier, now in the Federal Republic of Germany.

¶ The oldest and best is the fine Jesse Window in the chancel. It was made in the fourteenth century and was brought here in 1792 across the town from Old St. Chad's, in Belmont, having been transferred there from a Franciscan Friary. It was presented originally by Sir John Charlton of Powis and his wife.

PLACES OF INTEREST IN THE NEIGHBOURHOOD

64. Where a Stuntman had a Great Fall (Shrewsbury)
46. The Drunken Steeplejack (Shrewsbury)
55. Laura's Tower (Shrewsbury)
50. Grope Lane (Shrewsbury)

FOOD AND ACCOMMODATION

Good places, catering for all tastes, in the town.

67 The Cantlin Stone

POSITION: Bettws-y-Crwyn

ORDNANCE MAP: Landranger 137. Ludlow, Wenlock Edge etc.

MAP REF: SO202869

ACCESS: This is probably the most difficult to find of all our curiosities, being in a fenced enclosure in a field in a remote corner of the Clun Forest. The stone is marked on your map. Choose your day carefully if you decide to look for it. It can be bleak around those parts, and muddy underfoot after rain. But the open views are richly rewarding.

NOTE: The stone is said to be a cross marking the grave of William Cantlin, a pedlar who 300 years ago was murdered and robbed in that lonely spot. The men of Bettwys-y-Crwyn buried him. At the time of the Enclosures, when a dispute arose about the ownership of the land, the case was decided in favour of the parish of Bettws-y-Crwyn on the evidence of the stone.

¶ The cross stood some six feet high, carved stone on a stone base. Unhappily, it has collapsed, and the inscription is weathered and difficult to decipher. The accompanying information tablet is also hard to read, being in small, faint script. So if you want to learn more about this curious monument, take a magnifying glass!

PLACES OF INTEREST IN THE NEIGHBOURHOOD

14. The Shepherds' Church (Bettws-y-Crwyn Church)
68. Offa's Dyke (Mainstone)

FOOD AND ACCOMMODATION

Nothing out here. Clun is the nearest oasis, then Bishop's Castle.

68 Offa's Dyke

POSITION: Near Mainstone, in the Clun Forest

ORDNANCE MAP: Landranger 137. Ludlow, Wenlock Edge etc.

MAP REF: SO258896

ACCESS: There are very many places in the west of the county where you can clearly see the line of the bank and ditch. This one is on the unclassified road between Bishop's Castle and Newtown and precisely on the county boundary. At the above map reference, jump out of your car and look around you. You are barely on the edge, it seems, of civilization! The best method of keeping your bearings is for your navigator to count and check off the road junctions as you proceed.

NOTE: All schoolchildren know (don't they?) that the Dyke was built over several years in the early eighth century on the orders of Offa, King of Mercia, to mark the boundary between his territory and that of the marauding Welsh. The earthwork stretched originally 168 miles from Prestatyn to Chepstow, with some breaks, presumably where there was thick woodland. From our chosen viewpoint there are most impressive views across the valley into Wales.

PLACES OF INTEREST IN THE NEIGHBOURHOOD
59. A Quiet Church in a Quiet Town

FOOD AND ACCOMMODATION
Best take your own and have a picnic.

69 Laudian Candlesticks

POSITION: Lydbury North Church

ORDNANCE MAP: Landranger 137. Ludlow, Wenlock Edge etc.

MAP REF: SO528611

ACCESS: The village is on the B4385 road, three and a half miles south-east of Bishop's Castle.

NOTE: The Laudian candlesticks are wooden and baluster-shaped and stand on stone brackets above the high stone altar. William Laud was Archbishop of Canterbury during most of the 11 years when Charles I ruled without a Parliament. He imposed strict Anglican practices and religious uniformity. He was executed in 1644.

¶ The candlesticks represent a rare relic from about 1640, and were set up originally beside the altar instead of images.

PLACES OF INTEREST IN THE NEIGHBOURHOOD

52. The One-armed Clock (at the same church)
60. The Direction Pillar (Little Brampton)
59. A Quiet Church in a Quiet Town (Clun)

FOOD AND ACCOMMODATION

At Bishop's Castle, Clun or Craven Arms.

70 A Stonehenge Folly

POSITION: Weston Rhyn

ORDNANCE MAP: Landranger 126. Shrewsbury, etc.

MAP REF: SJ279363

ACCESS: From where the five lane-ends meet in the middle of the village, take the unclassified road leading northwards past the church for three-quarters of a mile. Just beyond the cemetery, find the footpath on your left which will take you through Temple Wood and leads past the 'Temple' itself, again on your left.

NOTE: One of the few follies in Shropshire is this imitation stone circle, made of stones and concrete, put up by a Major West, an eccentric landowner, in the last century. It is in the corner of a sloping field, with a wood on one side of it.
¶ Some local people find it fascinating, and describe it as a beauty spot, and have been known to refer to it as the Druid's Temple. The Major's motives for building it are not known.

PLACES OF INTEREST IN THE NEIGHBOURHOOD
9. Four Ways to Cross a Valley (Chirk)
33. Church Furniture of the Past (St. Martin's)
5. The Italian Station (Gobowen)
6. A Venerable Churchyard Yew (Dudleston)

FOOD AND ACCOMMODATION
In Chirk.

71 The Condover Memorials

POSITION: Condover Church

ORDNANCE MAP: Landranger 126. Shrewsbury, etc.

MAP REF: SJ495057

ACCESS: Leave the A49(T) road just south of Bayston Hill and the charming village of Condover is only a couple of miles away.

NOTE: The church dominates the settlement, but around a tight corner, and hugged by high walls, the way leads to the magnificent E-plan Elizabethan Hall, for some years now a school for handicapped children.

¶The sculptured monuments in the church are of varying styles and quality. They are mostly connected with the Owens, the Scrivens and the Cholmondleys, whose home was the Hall, and you might find it rewarding to study the inscriptions and the detail on the figures. Robert Owen's monument has been called theatrical; the more upright figures of Thomas and Alice Cholmondley are more natural.

¶Look up at the fine hammerbeam roof while you are there, and the lychgate is worth a second glance, too.

PLACES OF INTEREST IN THE NEIGHBOURHOOD

62. The Column (Shrewsbury)
13. A Modest Telford Bridge (Cantlop)
22. Acton Burnell Castle
3. The Parliamentary Gable Ends (Acton Burnell)
73. Burnell Burnished Brass (Acton Burnell)

FOOD AND ACCOMMODATION

Abounding in Shrewsbury.

72 Grinshill Quarries

POSITION: On Grinshill Hill, between the villages of Clive and Grinshill.

ORDNANCE MAP: Landranger 126. Shrewsbury, etc.

MAP REF: SJ525238

ACCESS: Drive up an approach lane from the unclassified Clive–Preston Brockhurst road at SJ528246 to the car park in Corbet Wood.

NOTE: Quarrying activity on this 'white' sandstone outcrop, 630 feet high, is only a shadow of what it used to be. The stone which was cut and hauled from these holes, 200 feet deep, was used to build, among many other things, parts of the Roman settlement of Uriconium, Crewe Railway Station, Attingham Hall, Shrewsbury's English Bridge, and—a curious distinction, this—the frame of No. 10, Downing Street.

¶ The old workings are but flimsily guarded with wooden fencing and wire.

PLACES OF INTEREST IN THE NEIGHBOURHOOD

58. A Van Gogh Canal Bridge (Tilstock)
40. The Church made Famous by a Shropshire Chronicler (Myddle)
32. The Bull Ring (Loppington)

FOOD AND ACCOMMODATION

Wem, Shrewsbury, or a village inn.

73 The Burnell Burnished Brass

POSITION: Acton Burnell Church

ORDNANCE MAP: Landranger 126. Shrewsbury, etc.

MAP REF: SJ533020

ACCESS: As for No. 22.

NOTE: The brass, a table tomb in the north transept, is only one of several remarkable monuments in this thirteenth-century church. It represents Sir Nichols Burnell, who died in 1382, in the armour of the period.
¶There are few good pictorial brasses in Shropshire. You would have to pay a fee if you wanted to rub this one.

PLACES OF INTEREST IN THE NEIGHBOURHOOD
3. The Parliamentary Gable Ends (Acton Burnell)
22. Acton Burnell Castle
30. Langley Chapel (Langley)

FOOD AND ACCOMMODATION
A wide choice at Shrewsbury, seven miles or so to the north.

74 The Rake's Progress

POSITION: 'The Mytton and Mermaid' Hotel at Atcham

ORDNANCE MAP: Landranger 126. Shrewsbury, etc.

MAP REF: SJ542092

NOTE: The most curious thing about Mad Jack Mytton, one of Shropshire's best-known eccentrics, is that he left nothing tangible in the county to which the story of his mercurial career can be attached. Only his name remains, in printed form in map and book, street sign and place-name.

¶ But his ghost is said to walk occasionally in this hotel, where his body lay on its last night above the earth. He was buried on the following day at the ancestral home at Halston Hall, near Whittington, within the precincts of the private black-and-white chapel. Nowadays, neither the hall nor the chapel is open to the public.

¶ Mytton was born rich, and dissipated all his wealth in riotous living, especially in drinking and gambling. He died in abject poverty, a sick and broken man, in Paris, at the age of 38. He was restless, wild, and immensely popular. Apart from the gaming table and the bottle, his greatest pleasures were derived from the traditional gentleman's sports of hunting, shooting and fishing, and from outrageous feats of daring.

¶ One of the best-known concerns Mytton's attempt to leap over the crossing-gates at Hanwood with a pony and trap. Yet another tells how he set fire to the tail of his own shirt in order to cure a severe attack of hiccups. (He suffered third degree burns, but the hiccups left him.)

PLACES OF INTEREST IN THE NEIGHBOURHOOD

16. The Scarfaced Effigy (Berrington)
18. Where the Severn is Double-crossed (Atcham)
13. A Modest Telford Bridge (Cantlop)

FOOD AND ACCOMMODATION

Shrewsbury is only four miles away.

75 The Refectory Pulpit

POSITION: Shrewsbury.

ORDNANCE MAP: Landranger 126. Shrewsbury, etc.

MAP REF: SJ498124

ACCESS: On Abbey Foregate, opposite the Abbey Church, on the other side of the road.

NOTE: When the ruins of the dissolved Benedictine Abbey were sold in 1810, the bit of land on which the refectory pulpit stands went to the parish, and it was still there, with its garden, when Telford's London–Holyhead road was laid down between it and the Abbey church.

¶The octagonal pulpit, of Grinshill stone, has been described as an architectural gem. It is supposed to date from the end of the fourteenth century—later than the Norman refectory itself—and would have been used by the duty monk for reading to his brothers, required to eat their meal without speaking.

¶The Benedictine Abbey, of which the pulpit formed an element, was the setting for the historical novels of Ellis Peters, in which the hero, Brother Cadfael, is the keeper of the herb garden and a successful sleuth.

PLACES OF INTEREST IN THE NEIGHBOURHOOD

62. The Column (Shrewsbury)
44. New St. Chad's (Shrewsbury)
64. Where a Stuntman had a Great Fall (Shrewsbury)
46. The Drunken Steeplejack (Shrewsbury)

FOOD AND ACCOMMODATION

Plentiful whichever way you go.

76 Where the Shropshire Lad at last found Peace

POSITION: St. Laurence's Church, Ludlow

ORDNANCE MAP: Landranger 137. Ludlow, Wenlock Edge etc.

MAP REF: SO520755

NOTE: The curious thing about the Shropshire Lad is that A. E. Housman, (1859-1936), classical scholar and popular poet, wasn't one. He was born near Bromsgrove, in Worcestershire, and spent most of his life in London and Cambridge.
¶Housman was a lonely man but his simple and nostalgic lyrical poems in 'A Shropshire Lad'—63 of them—were immensely popular during the first World War. He used an idealised Shropshire as his setting, and a soldier or a farmworker as the imagined speaker or listener.
¶His ashes were buried close to the north wall of the church, and a plaque low down in a recess bears his epitaph.

PLACES OF INTEREST IN THE NEIGHBOURHOOD
54. The Hexagonal Porch (Ludlow)
53. The Face at The Feathers (Ludlow)

FOOD AND ACCOMMODATION
In the town, which is a busy tourist port-of-call, especially in summer.

77 The Bell-ringers' Rules

POSITION: Church of St. Mary and St. Bartholomew, Tong

ORDNANCE MAP: Landranger 127. Stafford, Telford, etc.

MAP REF: SJ796074

ACCESS: Tong is close to the A41(T) road, some two and a half miles north of Albrighton.

NOTE: The bell-ringers' rules, written nearly 300 years ago, are to be found near the organ in the church, and provide an interesting and revealing comment on the village, church, and, indeed, social life of an English rural community of that period.

¶ Most of the village men could have belonged to the bell-ringing fraternity. The art, or craft, was taken very seriously. The tower captain, responsible for calling changes, maintaining of the ring, and discipline within the ringing chamber, would have been a man of some authority.

¶ As can be readily seen, forfeits were payable for inattention, incompetence, and lapses of decorum. A barrel of beer was generally on tap in the chamber to refresh the ringers after what would have been thirsty work.

¶ Do not miss the monumental treasures in this remarkable church.

PLACES OF INTEREST IN THE NEIGHBOURHOOD

7. The Matthew Webb Monument (Dawley)
79. The Mary Tooth Tomb (Madeley)

FOOD AND ACCOMMODATION

Available in Ludlow.

78 Oswald's Well

POSITION: Maserfield, Oswestry

ORDNANCE MAP: Landranger 126. Shrewsbury, etc.

MAP REF: SJ285292

ACCESS: On the left of the unclassified road to Trefonen, on the western edge of the town.

NOTE: Legend has it that King Oswald of Northumbria fought King Penda hereabouts in the year 642, and was defeated. When his body was dismembered (a barbaric but not uncommon practice in those times) an eagle swooped down and carried off an arm, which had been hung on a handy tree. The bird dropped the limb, however, and where it fell a spring welled up out of the ground.
¶In due course, the well was protected by a wall and a grating, and you could use a ladle attached by a chain to the ironwork to take a cool drink and make three wishes. The ladle is no longer there, probably on hygienic grounds. The well is maintained by the local town council.
¶Many people believe that the name Oswestry is a simple corruption of Oswald's Tree.

PLACES OF INTEREST IN THE NEIGHBOURHOOD

45. Old Oswestry
33. Church Furniture of the Past (St. Martin's)
9. Four Ways to Cross a Valley (Chirk)

FOOD AND ACCOMMODATION

The town is well-blessed with restaurants and public-houses.

79 The Mary Tooth Tomb

POSITION: See below, Access.

ORDNANCE MAP: Landranger 127. Stafford, Telford, etc.

MAP REF: SJ697041

ACCESS: The church is about half a mile south of the A4169, between Woodside and Sutton, but it's not particularly easy to find.

NOTE: There are several cast-iron tombs in the churchyard, forming fitting memorials to the early ironfounders and their families, who made the area famous. Near the churchyard entrance and well-nigh impossible to miss is the black table tomb to Mary Tooth, who died on November 15th, 1843, aged 65.

¶ She was the adopted daughter of the Fletchers, a name to conjure with hereabouts. The Rev. William Fletcher, of Swiss extraction, was the vicar of Madeley from 1760 to 1785, and was indefatigable among the motley ranks of workers in the new industries springing up in the Severn Gorge during those years. He devoted tremendous energy and goodwill to their welfare and to getting them to church. When he died, his wife carried on his good work. When *she* died, Mary carried on where her adoptive parents had left off.

PLACES OF INTEREST IN THE NEIGHBOURHOOD

7. The Matthew Webb Monument (Dawley)

FOOD AND ACCOMMODATION

Ample in Telford, which is nowadays considerably bigger than Shrewsbury.

80 The Cast-iron Canal Aqueduct

POSITION: Longdon on Tern

ORDNANCE MAP: Landranger 127. Stafford, Telford, etc.

MAP REF: SJ617156

ACCESS: Take the B5063 for Admaston from the A442 Telford–Whitchurch road. After half a mile, before Admaston, the B5063 bends right and reaches Longdon on Tern after a further two and a half miles or so. The aqueduct is in a field on your right.

NOTE: This rare monument to the Industrial Revolution was designed to carry the Shropshire Union Canal over the valley of the River Tern. It was originally 65 yards in length, and is the oldest aqueduct of its type in the world, having been built by Telford in about 1795.

¶ When the Shrewsbury branch of the canal network was dispensed with in 1967, the land was reclaimed for agriculture, and the aqueduct left high-and-dry in a field.

PLACES OF INTEREST IN THE NEIGHBOURHOOD

28. A Romantic Roofless Ruin (Moreton Corbet)
72. Grinshill Quarries (Grinshill Hill)

FOOD AND ACCOMMODATION

At Market Drayton.

Select Bibliography

Alcock. *Discovering Salop*, Shire Publications, 1975
Arrowsmith. *Rides 'n Walks*, Express & Star
Blackwall. *Historic Bridges of Shropshire*, Shropshire Libraries, 1985
Challenge. *St. Mary's Church, Burford*, Orphans Press, 1970
Davies. *Mare's Milk and Wild Honey*
Gibbons. *The Welsh Border*, Geographia
Greenswood. *Who's Buried Where in England?*, Constable, 1982
Hadfield. *The Canals of the West Midlands*, David & Charles, 1966
Headley & Meulenkamp. *Follies*, National Trust Guide, Cape, 1986
Herring. *Shropshire*, Elek, 1949
Jackson. *Castles of Shropshire*, Shropshire Libraries, 1988
Kissack. *The River Severn*, Lavenham Press, 1982
Malden. *Short Guide to the Church of St. Mary the Virgin, Cleobury Mortimer*
Mee. *Shropshire*, Hodder & Stoughton, 1939
Morton. *The Trees of Shropshire*, Airlife, 1986
Moulder. *Shropshire*, Shell Guide, Faber & Faber, 1951
Pearson's Canal Companion. *Llangollen and Shropshire Union*
Peel. *Portrait of the Severn*, Hale, 1968
Peters. *A Morbid Taste for Bones*, Futura, 1977
Pevsner. *Shropshire*, (The Buildings of England), Penguin, 1958
Salter. *The Castles and Moated Mansions of Shropshire*, Shropshire Libraries, 1988
Salter. *The Old Parish Churches of Shropshire*, Folly Publications, 1988
Trinder. *A History of Shropshire*, Phillimore, 1983
Trinder. *The Industrial Revolution in Shropshire*, Phillimore, 1973
Wren. *Shrewsbury & Shropshire*, Longmans, 1968

Bridgnorth, British Publishing Co. Ltd, Gloucester
Britain's Heritage, ed. Norwich, Granada, 1983
Country Quest magazine: various issues
Dictionary of British History, ed. Kenyon, Secker & Warburg, 1981
English Villages. ed. Hadfield, (Shell), Michael Joseph, 1980
Guide to Oswestry & District, ed. Evans
Shrewsbury Castle, Wilding
Shropshire, (S.C.C.), British Publishing Co. Ltd, Gloucester, 1988
Shropshire, (S.C.C.), 1980
South Shropshire, Official Guide, 1983
The Shropshire Village Book, (W.I.), Countryside Books, 1988

9 *Four Ways to Cross a Valley*